home a

children

pocket

Our so

is made

flour g

Pocket Bakery

D083O963

700040986075

pocket bakery

'The smell of good bread baking, like the sound of lightly flowing water, is indescribable in its evocation of innocence and delight.'

M.F.K. Fisher

The
Pocket
Bakery

Rose Prince is an acclaimed food journalist and writer. She has been writing and campaigning for good food for over 15 years and writes a column for the *Daily Telegraph*, also contributing to *The Independent, Daily Mail, Spectator* and the Radio 4 *Food Programme*. She is the author of three bestselling cookery books, *The New English Kitchen, The New English Table* and *Kitchenella*. Since launching the Pocket Bakery in 2010, she created *Rose Prince's Baking Club* – a forum for recipes, reader tips and advice, which is featured every Saturday in the *Telegraph Weekend*. She lives in London and Dorset with her husband, Dominic Prince, and their two children.

Delicious breads, cakes and pastries from a family bakery

The Pocket Bakery

Rose Prince

WEIDENFELD & NICOLSON

Introduction

It was never the plan for the bakery to become what it is, to play the role it has. It was only about children earning a bit of pocket money, so we called it the Pocket Bakery. That was three years ago, and the bakery has grown from two children selling a few loaves from our kitchen door in south London, to a blossoming business with a place on the shelves of the city's oldest and most famous food hall. Yet this is not just a success story; it is also about how the bakery unexpectedly transformed the life of one child, turning it around from disappointment to triumph.

The bakery became a place of apprenticeship for my son Jack, who was 14 when the bakery opened, and is now 18. He left school at 16 and began training as a professional baker and for the Pocket Bakery. It is very much down to him that the bakery is where it is today.

The first year – pocket money
This element was unexpected, because the beginnings of the bakery were so minuscule. We first talked about it in the summer of 2010. It came out of one of those conversations about money, not without its heated moments. When your children hit their teenage years, you hear the words 'I need...' almost daily. Those 'needs' are amplified for children constantly confronted by the attractions of a metropolis like London, and especially unequal to mine at the same age, growing up in 1970s rural England.

My husband Dominic and I ruefully anticipated years of demands; with Jack aged 14 and Lara 11, we were only at the beginning of the era of being a familial cash machine. Attempts to make pocket money a reward for help in the house always failed, no matter how many duty rotas I stuck to the fridge door. As it was, my heart was not really in paying children to do things

I thought they should do unasked. The more I thought about them using a skill to make a little cash, the more sense it made. 'Why not bake bread to sell to the neighbours?' I said. 'We don't know how to make bread,' they said. In truth, neither did I – at least, not the kind of traditional sourdough breads I thought would be marketable. The only thing I had going for the plan was a large gas oven in my kitchen, built for catering, that could take five loaves at a time.

Deciding the children's response to the idea was not exactly a 'no', I held on to the thought that we would do it one day. I gave it a working title, the Pocket Bakery, which also helped keep the scheme alive. But it was six months before we made a single loaf and in the end it happened because I met the person we like to call the 'father of the bakery', Giuseppe Mascoli. Giuseppe not only gave us the first vital bread-making lesson, he gave us a very special ingredient,

the 'mother', or sourdough starter, that would leaven the bread.

The mother

As we made plans for the bakery, from the outset we agreed it was important to sell bread that had a higher value. In other words, our bread would be made using the best flour available, and be made using a slow fermentation method – the type of bread known as 'sourdough'. The children did not know what I was on about. They had seen me make buns and pizza using shop-bought fast-action yeast, but sourdough bread-making was a mystery to them. I knew little more about it myself, aside from having enjoyed eating such bread which, like handmade cheese or vintage wine, has a superior flavour and texture compared to its commercial equivalents.

I explained to the children that to make delicious, great-textured, long-lasting bread you do not use fast-action yeast but instead

add a small amount of previously fermented dough, called the 'mother' or 'sourdough starter', to the mix. You must refresh or feed the mother with more flour and water regularly, to keep it alive and active so it will leaven the bread and give it a good flavour. Sourdough is unpredictable, I said, telling them the little I knew. Compared to commercial yeast it is very slow to act – so breads like these can take a minimum of 15 hours to develop and expand with bubbles before being ready to bake. Seeing their horrified faces picturing hours of graft, I hastily added that for the vast majority of that time the baker need do nothing at all – the dough is left alone to prove, or ferment.

Giuseppe

I met Giuseppe Mascoli (pictured above left) in July 2010 in London. A former lecturer in economics, impassioned baker and the originator of London's best pizzeria chain, Franco Manca, he is happiest plotting new food businesses when not socialising in any place where the food and drink is good. He also has in his possession a sourdough 'mother', known to have been 'alive' and in use since 1790, which his bakers use in the commercial bakery he co-runs, and in Franco Manca where it is used to leaven the pizza dough. The yeasts and acids in the starter are unknown, but the benefits they give to the bread in terms of texture and flavour are exceptional.

Giuseppe was born in Positano near Naples. His childhood was spent in the multi-pastel-coloured coastal village built on a cliff face. Even if overrun with tourists, Positano remains one of the world's great romantic hotspots; my parent spent their honeymoon there in the 1950s, and it still swarms with couples, traipsing hand in hand through its tiny streets.

The Mascoli family home in Positano is high on the hill overlooking the Amalfi Coast and outlying islands. A bakery on one of

these, Ischia, is the place where Giuseppe's 'mother' (sourdough starter) originated. Of course, you have to question its authenticity, since it seems almost unbelievable that a piece of fermented food can last that long. Travelling there with Dominic in 2012, we asked Giuseppe if it was really possible for a piece of fermented dough to have been alive for that long.

He pointed to the rocky cliffs that rise high above the villages on the coast. 'Look at the landscape here: there are many villages which would have been mostly cut off from the rest of the mainland, except for occasional sea transport. It was in the interests of the bakers on the islands and coastal villages to look after the mother, so they could always make bread and be self-sufficient.'

The sourdough may be even older. 'The bakery in Ischia has it on record that it has been in use since 1790, but the bakers say there is no reason why it cannot date back to Roman times,' he said.

When I told Giuseppe that we wanted to start a bakery in our home, he was immediately enthusiastic and offered to show us how to make sourdough bread. This is very typical of this wonderful and generous-spirited man. 'Children making sourdough for a bakery business – fantastic!' he said. We set a date to begin, in mid-November 2010.

The first bread

We chose to make bread on Fridays, starting after both children returned from school and leaving it to prove overnight so it was ready to be baked and then sold on Saturday morning. As the day approached, on Giuseppe's instructions, I bought a few basic pieces of equipment. 'Don't buy professional stuff, just improvise – as you know, they might not keep at it.' I fully expected them both to give up after a short

time myself, but I did not imagine that they would not turn up at all.

At 3pm Giuseppe was at the door, having arrived on his motorbike. In his hand was a plastic container, containing a few hundred grams of the mother. I had ordered an 8-kilogram bag of strong white flour from Cann Water Mill in north Dorset. Stoate's Flour is milled in this historic place by Michael Stoate and we believe it to be the finest you can buy for the purpose. The organic strong white flour is British and stone-milled before being sieved to remove the bran. The natural oils released in the milling stay in the flour and bread made with it tends not to be white but buff coloured.

By the time we were ready to make the dough, the children had returned from school. Both made their excuses, saying they had urgent things they needed to do with friends. They exchanged a look that said 'My God she was actually serious!' and disappeared. Giuseppe taught me the basics of mixing a sourdough that evening (he would be pestered with desperate phone enquiries from me in the weeks to come) but by 10pm I had ten pieces of dough, each wrapped in a couche cloth (floured cloth), ready to prove (leave to rise) overnight.

The next morning the children both stayed in their beds while I went down to bake. I burnt at least half of the bread that morning, at least the underside of it. The one piece of equipment I did not buy, and which is essential for baking breads made with wet-textured dough, is a baking stone. The stone, which is like a thin fireproof ceramic tile, is placed in the oven before baking to heat. The bread is baked directly on it instead of a baking sheet and the stone keeps the base crust crisp without letting it burn.

A first lesson learned the hard way, yet I sold seven loaves to friends I had invited to the bakery, and later waived my earnings, a £20 note, at the children. There was a spark of interest, and the following week both printed out one hundred flyers, giving our address and illustrated with a little pocket full of bread logo, which we are still using today. They walked around the neighbourhood, pushing them through letterboxes.

Both helped make the bread on the second Friday, mixing several kilos of dough together in a large plastic box you would normally buy as a mothproof store-box for woollens, and then kneaded it on the kitchen table. Giuseppe brought us four untreated quarry tiles to use as baking stones in the oven and when the bread came out of the oven the next morning it looked – well – rather professional.

Customers

That feeling when you open up shop for the first and the very first customer comes through the door – a stranger – is very special. For us the surprise was that it is not just the satisfaction in selling a loaf of the bread, but the short conversation that took place with a neighbour we had never before met. It is a sad fact that we had lived in our home for fifteen years and yet knew hardly anyone in our street except those living immediately next door.

That second Saturday morning, aside from having been a successful day's trading (the children took £45), was the moment we unearthed a community of wonderful people. I realise now that it took a little courage on the part of our customers to ring the bell of someone's home. When you enter a shop you keep your anonymity, but buying bread from someone's kitchen means even a small chat is inescapable.

Names were exchanged as Dominic collected email addresses for a weekly mailing – he had the good idea that our customers could pre-order as it would give us some idea of how much to make each week. Little enquiries were made by our shyer Battersea people, and we learned tiny bits about their lives. Others were more effusive – by their third visit to the bakery we were greeted with a kiss on the cheek by some.

There was the artist, Phil, who painted beautiful landscapes and later lent my daughter one of his sketchbooks to help with her art homework. Always our earliest customer, he would knock on the door within moments of our 9am opening, usually as we were cooking breakfast. Like Dominic he was a sausage and black pudding aficionado, and soon brought us porky things he had found in different butchers' shops that he thought were good to try. He introduced us to another neighbour, a vibrant Greek artist, Monika, who then introduced us to her daughter, who became another regular.

There was Susan, who lived just a few doors away, a passionate hiker and lover of the countryside who would buy bread before setting off to stomp over heathland, and the super-fit women with glowing faces who had done their Saturday morning yoga class together and more often bought our wholesome 100 per cent rye bread. We also sold to what became known as the South East Sales Division, a family who would buy about 15 loaves and distribute them to their own neighbours in Camberwell. News of the bread was spreading – and our email list grew to over a hundred.

We came to know Victoria, a beautiful young city worker with a glossy black dog called Bella. She began walking our own dog Billy, and would look after him if we went away for the odd night. One weekend

she arrived on the doorstep in floods of tears, telling us that Bella had been taken by strangers while being walked in Battersea Park. I was baking with the children that Friday and we sat up into the small hours fretting and trying to calm her down, with, it must be said, copious quantities of wine.

Both children were deeply upset on her behalf, even though they had known her only for a matter of weeks. Because of the bakery, our neighbours' anxieties had become ours, as well as the other customers who heard about it. When her dog Bella was returned to her, everyone connected to the bakery celebrated.

Through Victoria we met Anita, who kept bantams on the roof of her Battersea house. When they laid more than usual she brought surplus eggs to the bakery and we would sell them for her. She kept a number of other extraordinary animals in her house, including rats and reptiles which

she would take around to show children in local schools. When another customer came in to collect bread, bemoaning a long bike journey she needed to make that day to buy live grasshoppers to feed her child's chameleon, we called Annette, who came round carrying a Tetrapak box reverberating with the sound of jumping insects.

Our friends became loyal customers, and the bakery an opportunity to see people regularly who I might only see once every few weeks, even months. Great was the day when a customer arrived at noon to pick up bread and was still there at five in the afternoon, chatting. Too often work and family made it impossible to have much of a social life, yet the bakery combined these elements. I may not have been earning much from the bakery, but the children, who were earning up to £50 per week, thought the rewards were rich. For me the venture had other bonuses.

The second year – Jack

Running their own small business did more than make our children richer in cash terms. They took pride in earning their own, and it gave them more freedom and the ability to choose to do things they dreamed about. Lara saved enough to pay half of the cost towards a school sports trip to South Africa that we would never have been able to pay for in full. In addition to saving for her trip through the Pocket Bakery, she and her friends took up baking more cakes to raise separate funds to buy sports equipment for some of the Township schools they would be visiting. I was full of pride – all of us describe their age group as selfish, yet here was proof they are anything but.

At the time, both children attended a day school in Battersea. 'What's this about a bakery?' one of the teachers asked me at a parents' evening. I am not sure they approved, as if the bakery was eating into precious time that could be spent doing homework. But it was not, and in Jack's case it would not have mattered if it did.

By the summer of 2012, one year and a half after opening, the Pocket Bakery had another job to do, and I write about this in retrospect, because Jack is now 18 and is happy for me to do so. We also believe he is an inspiration to other children like him who for some reason feel they do not fit the orthodox path of childhood.

By then we knew that Jack was one of those children who did not fit into conventional education. He is exceptionally bright and talented but, as many children find, he could not cope with the pressures and disciplines of the first secondary school he attended and began to get into trouble.

When the school asked him to leave aged 13 it was a great shock, and his confidence was shattered. The effect of being rejected by his educators and de facto losing the friends he

had spent nearly two years with had severe consequences. While the next two schools he attended were more understanding, he was by this time uninspired.

A period of home education was not a success and by September 2011 it was obvious that to continue would make a troubled boy worse. We decided that schooling had to end, or at least go on hold, and Jack found himself in the altogether more daunting adult world.

He had very little money and no qualifications, but he did have his little bakery business. It did not do everything to restore his self-esteem, however, and being open once a week was not enough to keep Jack busy. In his own words he describes that time:

'I had little to do apart from roam the streets of south London and my parents were at their wits' end. I was continuously drifting and my behaviour was becoming more and more reckless. It was a period in my life when I felt really down. I was not at school – but I was at least baking.'

An encounter with another bakery based in Oxfordshire changed everything for Jack. 'The turning point for me came in May 2012 when I went with my mum to give a breadmaking demonstration at Daylesford, the organic farm shop in Gloucestershire owned by Carole Bamford. After the demonstration Carole asked me if I would like a job in her wholesale bakery. That was a truly monumental breakthrough. I packed my cases and went to live and work at Daylesford under the watchful eye of Eric Duhamel, the chief baker.

'I had my own room in a lovely farmhouse, made some great friends and earned some really good money. Also my grandmother lived nearby and used to come and visit. I learned so much at Daylesford that I was

determined to pursue a career as a baking entrepreneur. I got a renewed sense of values, particularly for money. Baking was a constant in my life, in a way that school had not been.'

The period training with Eric Duhamel honed Jack's skills to a new level that he was able to bring back to the Pocket Bakery when he returned in September 2012. I realise now that while our bread had quality in terms of the sourdough and the flour we used, we lacked understanding about other processes, especially the kneading and shaping of the dough. Because of Jack, the standard of the bread improved greatly. Instead of a low-profile worthy appearance, the look of the loaves blossomed, looking structured, handsome and appetising; the interior crumb, once dense, was now filled with beautiful air bubbles. Suddenly our bread no longer looked like the work of enthusiastic amateurs, but professional.

The inspiration Jack found in his own enterprise and through baking bread has shown the extraordinary difference that acquiring a skill can make to school-age children who are not inspired by the conventional school curriculum. The educators may look down on any subject that does not impress a university entrance board, but then they fail to understand that industry is multi-faceted and the service industry is crucial in a highly populated nation. But then again, you only have to eat a school meal to know that conventional educators are limited in their abilities to teach quality of life.

How might the hospitality and food industry benefit if, instead of waiting for students to 'fail' at school, artisan skills such as slow fermentation and sourdough bread-making were taught before the age of 16, pre-empting the difficulties unconventional children face? Now that the Pocket Bakery is due to expand, Jack's struggles and the

way in which he has overcome some of them ('I am not there yet,' he will say), made us resolve to offer apprenticeships to other young people. The artisan bread industry is still small, and there is room for everyone.

The Doodle Bar

While Jack was training at Daylesford, we had discovered another Battersea secret. Down by Battersea Bridge, behind the Royal College of Art, there is a red-brick building that was once a dairy depot with huge refrigerated storage and room for the milk floats that once delivered milk all over the borough. Now it is called Testbed 1, an arts centre and office space, and at its heart is the Doodle Bar.

So called because the walls are painted blackboards and the college students who drink there doodle all over them when they meet up, the Doodle Bar is tucked away on the edge of Ransome's Dock, an inlet off the Thames. A small lane leads into the

building, and though it is a five-minute walk from my home, I did not hear about it until it had been open for some years. One day Dominic walked down to the bar and talked to the manager, Jasmin Ford, who was keen to find ways to bring more people into the bar during the day.

In May 2012, just as Jack left to work at the bakery in Gloucestershire, we decided to move the Pocket Bakery down to the Doodle Bar and open on Friday instead of Saturday. As well as bread we would make cakes and pies; a lunchtime trade we had not tried before. It was sad to close the Saturday bakery, but I now had to do the Doodle Bar lunch alone – Lara obviously could not work on school days.

The Doodle Bar has been a much greater test for the Pocket Bakery. Potentially there are many more customers but they can choose to buy lunch from a number of local businesses. Inside Testbed 1 there is

the Street Kitchen, which cooks great grills, vegetable dishes and salads, all of which are based on the finest British ingredients. A following for the Pocket Bakery pies and cakes has grown, however. Some of our regulars have followed us from the home bakery, and we have found new regulars. Being open on (ostensibly) the last working day of the week means that there is a festival atmosphere on many Fridays with people of all ages. In school holidays parents bring their children who scribble all over the walls, and it feels as if, through good food, the Battersea family is growing week by week.

The third year – West End

In the summer of 2012, we supplied bread and cake to a street party in Battersea held in celebration of Queen Elizabeth II's Diamond Jubilee. We created the Battersea Bridge Roll (page 81) to mark the event, and the Jammy Roll Cake (page 206), which we called a Saxe-Coburg cake on the occasion. The day was blissful; we drank English Nye Timber champagne and chefs Margot Henderson and Valentine Warner made asparagus soup and barbecued Coronation Chicken. One attendee at the street party, shortly to move to Battersea, was Ewan Venters, the newly appointed chief executive officer of Fortnum & Mason. When he tried the white sourdough, he suggested we might one day supply them.

In March 2013, Fortnum & Mason invited the Pocket Bakery to 'pop up' for two weeks, running a small café on the first floor and selling our breads. We arranged for the bakery in Brixton, run by Giuseppe Mascoli, to make four breads to our recipes and deliver the bread directly to the shop. The bread was displayed in the basement food hall, and Jack spent time there with a board covered in samples. He loves talking to people about the bread – explaining how it is made, all about the flour and the sourdough and why such breads need to cost a little more.

Three years on and so much has changed. The bakery, set up simply to earn a little cash and smooth the choppy waters that parents and children travel together, has done much more. Bringing together a neighbourhood, giving a troubled young person a purpose that had been absent before we made a single loaf and creating something that has won praise from the highest level. That all this comes from bread, the stuff of life, is perhaps not surprising. We just forget, from time to time, how important the simple things can be.

Rose Prince, November 2013

Baking basics

A few basic gadgets and pieces of kitchenware are helpful, even invaluable, for successful baking. It is also important to know how fitted equipment, like ovens, will adapt to the recipes you use.

Scales. I recommend using electronic scales for accuracy and also because you can weigh directly into mixing bowls, reducing the quantity of equipment – and washing-up. Professional baker's scales are more expensive but can weigh quantities of several kilograms.

Other measuring equipment. To prevent uncertainty, visit a kitchenware specialist for clear glass or Perspex measuring jugs with detailed measurements marked inside and outside. Measuring spoons are better than using domestic teaspoons and tablespoons, whose volume varies depending on design. Keep a ruler or tape measure handy in the kitchen for measuring bakeware.

Ovens: temperature. The recipes in this book have been tested in an oven that has had its temperature checked with a separate oven thermometer. Users of fan ovens should usually decrease the temperature by 10–20°C, but it must be said that the thermostats in domestic ovens vary greatly and cooks often learn to adapt, making adjustment themselves.

Ovens: humidity. Humidity in the oven helps to produce a crisp outer crust. Gas ovens and wood-fired ovens contain natural humidity, and to a degree so do Agas. But ordinary electric ovens produce a dry heat. Putting a shallow dish of boiling water in an electric oven will not make much difference as the steam largely escapes. Some new (very expensive) d mestic ovens can be connected to the water supply, as can some types of pizza oven. The best recommendation for electric baking is to use an ovenproof ceramic dome to place over the loaf as it bakes, creating a micro-climate around it that is hot and humid. These are available from artisan bakery suppliers – but a large casserole dish functions just as well. The dome must, however, be large enough to allow the bread to rise to its fullest.

Baking stones. Fireproof tiles or a 'pizza stone' heated in the oven make a natural surface on which to bake bread or pastry that prevent burning on the underside yet will ensure it is crisp. You will need a baker's 'peel', which resembles a large aluminium paddle – both items are available from pizzeria equipment suppliers.

Refrigeration and proving dough. A thermometer for the outdoors and indoors is recommended. Many of the breads in this book are slowly fermented and we have found this works best at a lower temperature than room temperature – about 14–16°C. The average temperature of a domestic fridge is between 1 and 5 degrees Celsius, which is too low except for certain types of dough – though you can prove dough for 24–36 hours in the fridge and produce a great loaf, if rather slowly. If you know the temperature indoors or outside it makes it easier to predict how long dough needs to prove (or develop and rise). Sometimes we put dough in well-protected containers outdoors to prove, but if it is too cold in the garden, a shed can be useful. In mid-winter the temperature in the kitchen at night can be low enough. In high summer it is inevitable that the bread-making process will be shorter. See the seasonal proving chart on page 31.

Bakeware. With the right equipment, you can try almost anything. There are ways of improvising to keep costs low when testing the enjoyment of baking – don't go and buy the full plethora of gadgetry if you are unsure if baking is for you. When we started the Pocket Bakery, we made the bread in giant containers normally used for storing blankets to protect them from moths. After a year we found an online supplier of professional baker's vats with lids. They will last us years but, remember, what you use has very little impact on the taste of what you make. At the back of this book is a list of suppliers who can provide lovely items like linen-lined baskets for proving bread, special blades (lames) for scoring loaves, peels, domes, 'couche' cloths, electronic thermometers and scales and even wood-fired ovens.

COOK'S NOTES

The price of baking

The costs for professional bakers are set to rise sharply due to the cost of fuel and, in some countries, a change in climate. The impact has been seen in the considerable rise in the price of baked goods. It makes baking at home all the more sensible, even though you will feel the price rise, too. If you have storage space, buying in bulk cuts costs. Buy bulk baking ingredients from online suppliers (page 246) – who charge delivery – or from local cash and carry stores, who sell a good range of basics. Some foods are worth paying more for.

Measurements

Unless stated:

- All tablespoon and teaspoon quantities are level.

- 1 tablespoon measures 15ml and 1 teaspoon 5ml.

- A 'nut' of butter equals 1 level tablespoon.

- A pinch equals 2g/¼ teaspoon and yet is still approximate.

- Bite-sized means the size of the top joint of your forefinger/thumb.

- Cake and loaf tin sizes may be changed (within reason) but avoid overflows or very thin cakes. To deal with the latter, increase the recipe by half again. Line smaller tins with baking parchment that will cope with overflow.

Ingredients

Unless stated:

- Eggs are medium-sized free-range British.*

- Butter is unsalted British* or French.

- Dried yeast is 'easy-bake' or 'quick' commercial yeast granules (no need to dissolve).

- Fresh yeast is commercial compressed yeast (must be kept refrigerated).

- Vanilla extract is natural – not 'essence' containing the artificial flavouring, vanillin.

- Milk is whole (full fat).

- Water is from cold tap (bottled in regions where tap water is non-drinkable).

- Olive oil is extra virgin olive oil.

- Vegetable oil is either sunflower, grapeseed or groundnut oil.

- Fresh meat is free range or naturally reared British.*

- Salt is fine sea salt, or rock salt, unless specified.

- Black pepper is freshly ground.

* British ingredients are optional but specified partly because buying British supports UK producers. It can also, in the case of eggs, be a case of food safety. All eggs produced in Britain are stamped with the 'Red Lion' mark that guarantees the hens that laid them are vaccinated against salmonella. This means they may be safely used raw in icings and sauces, although – should you be selling such foods to the public – environmental health inspectors may insist you use pasteurised egg yolks or whites for such purposes. Always look at labels for the origins of fresh ingredients, and details about welfare; 'free-range' standards vary.

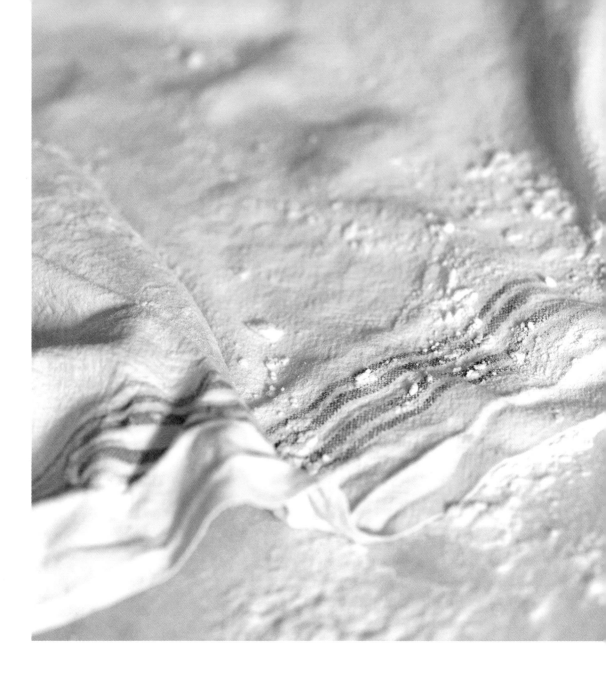

THE MIND OF A BAKER

Good bakers are forgiving and patient and become accustomed to the nuances of the craft. We have good and bad days; the elements interfere and we are fallible. Essentially we are all life-long apprentices; we never stop learning. We think that is why we love it this much.

The quantities and methods in this book are tried and tested but the outcome of any recipe may depend on unpredictable or outside forces, such as varying oven temperatures or the differing quality or properties of the ingredients you use. For example, not all butter is the same, so in certain recipes the type to use is specified.

Equipment, or the lack of it, can also have an impact on the result. Sometimes human error can enter the equation. Many times I have been on the point of putting a cake in the oven, even one I make regularly, only for it to occur to me that I might have forgotten to add the baking powder so clearly listed in the recipe.

This all amounts to the fact that a good baker is not made just by the recipes but by attitude. Your opinion and judgement play an important part. Creating that mind-set is a matter of following four precious rules:

Create calm. Find a time to bake when you have the best chance of concentrating – not while making supper, engrossed in another task or running around after family. Encourage children not to chatter when trying something for the first time – we find loud-ish music a brilliant way to help with concentration.

Avoid chaos. Keep tidy. Store baking ingredients together, making sure they are clearly labelled and so quick to find. Before starting, clear the worktops. Then always gather together every ingredient you need, so nothing will be forgotten, and choose and prepare bakeware.

Take control. You are not just a robot programmed by a recipe but gifted with valuable senses. Don't take cooking times for granted; use your eyes, nose, taste, touch and even your hearing to make judgements – the recipes in this book will encourage this.

Bounce back. If it 'goes wrong', remember bakers are forever cadets. We never stop being pupils, and mistakes and failures always improve us. Accentuate the positives: bad results may look a mess, but they are often still delicious.

Sourdough

Our bakery began with a very special loaf made to a tradition that has been handed down through centuries. In many ways it is an easier, not trickier bread to make than those with modern, commercially available ingredients. Traditional basic bread-making uses fewer ingredients and it needs less labour. Most significantly, its great texture and taste cannot be replicated without one remarkable ingredient: so-called 'sourdough', the natural leaven containing wild yeasts that gives this bread its life.

Sourdough is a strange term and something of a contradiction. It can be off-putting to first-time bakers who think the whole process too mysterious and an adventure likely to end in a nasty-tasting home brew. Nor does the name properly describe the flavour of a good sourdough, which, far from being sour enough to make you pull a face, is delicately ripe and wheaty, as if the flavour of the living plant has been distilled back into the bread.

There are many great books explaining the origins and science surrounding sourdoughs. When I tried to clarify and describe all this at the outset of the Pocket Bakery, the children's faces fell, just as mine does when a winemaker relates the chemical changes as

wine is made. Much as I love wine, I struggle with the scholarly details of its creation. Of course I respect the academics who labour to explain the subject but, especially when working with school-age children who are lesson-averse, we found it better to get down to making it and enjoying it and to acquire know-ledge through practical experience. The knowledge will come as your skills grow.

Almost from the first week we began to make our sourdough bread it was a pleasure. Oddly, once you start to make bread this way it seems to tell you what to do. This might sound crazy but bakers often talk about listening to dough. The experience gained after making bread just once or twice will naturally lead you to tweak the method or timing instinctively in order to make a better loaf that works in your environment.

We always say that a baker uses every sense when making sourdough. You touch dough that has been kneaded and rested and feel its liveliness and elasticity; a press with the finger can reveal if a loaf is ready to be baked. You can also, however, sense that it feels tight and unwieldy when overworked, which says it needs some resting time before kneading it further. You can sniff the dough and know that the fermentation is under way, or peer at it looking for developing air bubbles.

Soon you will know everything about bread-making and yet much of this will have come from you and not a recipe. Using our own experience we will give you every tip we can remember, and help to problem-solve. When you decide to make a sourdough, it is a commitment to a little trial and error, and it would be dishonest to say otherwise.

So don't be afraid to get into sourdough bread-baking. After all, you are only responsible for several million micro-organisms ... Seriously, the sourdough 'starter' we use to make these breads is not an animal, let alone a pet, but it is a live ingredient that must be kept fresh through regular feeds of water and flour. The bread-making itself is not rushed – the bread takes a minimum of 12 hours, though it is worth hastening to add that your input, in terms of labour, is a tenth of this time.

The burning question on a fledgling baker's mind will of course be, 'Where can I buy a sourdough starter?' The answer is that you rarely can. Professional bakers may part with a little, but some are protective as they regard the sourdough as the secret of their success. They may, if the sourdough has been alive for a long period of time, believe it has a very high value and wish to keep it under wraps.

This is all debatable. Some of the very oldest sourdoughs kept alive by traditional bakeries over decades, or even centuries, impart wonderful flavour and texture to bread, but unless they are well looked after they will not thrive. In other words, a sourdough starter is as good as the person who is responsible for it, and, just as with wine, every place will produce sourdough bread with its own special character.

If you have a friend who makes natural breads successfully, ask them for some starter – you only need 20 grams to get started and as you will discover (see page 34), most people with a starter in the home will have to throw some away each week as they have more than they need. Alternatively, make your own.

MAKING YOUR OWN SOURDOUGH STARTER

Begin with organic, stoneground rye flour. The wholesomeness of the base ingredient is important. Rye, a type of wheat, is the best for accelerating fermentation because it contains natural yeasts that quickly become active and tend also to give bread a good flavour. Note that liquid is nearly always weighed in bread-making, instead of measured by volume.

First day

Put 100g/3½oz rye flour in a clean bowl that you have previously washed out with boiling water. Add 70g/2½oz cold water from the tap and mix to a sticky paste. Put in a roomy plastic container (previously rinsed with boiling water), scatter some rye flour over the surface and cover with a tight-fitting lid. Do not put in a glass jar because glass can crack when the ferment creates gases. Place in a warm room, between 25 and 29°C, and leave for 4 days.

Fourth day

You will notice the contents of the container have become active, with small bubbles disturbing the surface. Sniff the starter – you will smell a slight ripeness.

Discard half of the fermenting starter and 'refresh' the rest, adding another 70g/2 ½oz rye flour and 40g/1 ½oz water. Mix to a wet paste (add more water if it is too stiff). Put into a clean roomy container, rinsed with boiled water, scatter a thin layer of flour on the surface, cover and leave for one day.

Fifth day

Repeat, discarding half the dough and refreshing with the same quantity of flour and water as for the fourth day.

Sixth day – the day of reckoning

By this time, your dough should be quite active. If not, just keep refreshing daily for up to 3 more days. It is ready to use when it bubbles up and increases in size within 5 hours of refreshment.

Now all this sounds easy, if demanding on patience, but unfortunately you cannot predict the flavour of a newly made sourdough. If your sourdough tastes ripe, slightly acidic and wheaty, and above all smells pleasant, it should impart a good flavour to bread. If, however, the mixture has an acrid or rotten smell, it is due to 'rogue' yeasts in the atmosphere that have infected the sourdough, and at this stage it would be better to throw it away and start again. Perhaps try another brand of rye flour, or mix it with a little wholemeal spelt or traditionally milled wholemeal flour. Alternatively, create different circum-stances, mixing it in another part of the home. Some bakers add a tablespoon of live yoghurt to sourdough, claiming it controls the bad yeasts.

To care for your starter, once it is active and bubbles up within hours when refreshed, see pages 34–35. You can keep the starter as a rye starter, or refresh it with white flour, ideal for making white breads.

Most sourdough bakers keep just one type of starter for breads made with different flours. This is the easiest policy for novice bakers. We use a starter refreshed with white flour for all our white breads, and a rye starter to make rye breads. But don't worry, either type can be used in any bread. For those who like their rye bread to contain only rye and no other type of wheat, a starter based on rye is the most suitable.

Artisan baking websites sell dried powder sourdough (see Suppliers, page 246). Backferment, a product ideal for making rye bread, is easy to activate (with water) and is unique in that after it has fermented you do not need to refresh it often so long as you keep it in the fridge.

Temperature

The temperature outside and inside your home determines the speed at which sourdough will prove. The rule is that the longer the ferment, the better the texture and flavour of the finished bread.

There are two ways to slow down the ferment: use less sourdough starter, or lower the proving temperature. Or both. The following is an approximate guide to the proving time for wheat bread (rye bread needs less – see page 48). Start times are suggested to be practical for those who want to bake in the morning – except for the 25°C prove, which can be achieved within a day. The temperature range shown below can be that inside your home or outdoors. We often prove outdoors, placing the loaves in a container with the lid weighted down to protect it from wildlife.

Celsius	Mix dough	Shape dough	2nd prove	Bake
25–30	9–10am	1–2pm	7 hours	8–9pm
15–20	3–4pm	7–8pm	9–10 hours	6–7am
10–15	2–3pm	5.30–6.30pm	11–12 hours	6–7am
5–10	1pm	5–6pm	14 hours	6–7am

Tip

If you bake a lot of bread, e.g. more than 6 loaves, keep waiting loaves in a cool place so they do not over-prove while other loaves are baked.

CARING FOR A SOURDOUGH STARTER

Once your sourdough starter is ready to use, you will need to keep it healthy and refresh it regularly. To refresh the starter, all you need to do is add flour and water and let it ferment and become active. If you do not refresh it, the starter will begin to produce acids and smell unpleasantly sour. If it is regularly refreshed then stored in the fridge in a clean plastic container covered by a lid, it should smell ripe and fruity and look active and bubbly.

....

Refreshing the starter
Note that the water is weighed. Use cold water from the mains tap.

Equipment
Plastic container **with lid**
Food-safe **gloves** (optional)

Ingredients
50g/1¾oz **starter**
50g/1¾oz **water**
100g/3½oz **organic flour**

....

Wash your hands, or when handling the starter wear 'food-safe' plastic gloves.

Prepare the new container by washing it and then sterilising it by pouring a kettle of boiling water inside and over the inside of the lid. Never use anti-bacterial cleaner or it can kill the starter.

Remove all but 50g/1¾oz of the starter in the existing container. Place the container on the scales and add the water. Stir with a stainless steel spoon to soften the starter so it is easier to add the flour. Add the flour and mix to a dough.

Pick up the dough with your hands, picking every bit off the container, then mix and knead with your hands until you have a sticky dough. If it is too wet, add extra flour.

When you have a smooth ball, place it in the new, clean container and put on the lid. Leave out of the fridge for about 4–6 hours. The warmer the temperature is, the faster the fermentation. Then, if you are not using it, put it in the fridge.

....

Further refreshments if NOT making bread with the starter

Your starter will now weigh 200g/7oz. You will need to refresh it regularly, even if you are not making bread with it. To refresh if not using, throw three-quarters of it away (or give it away) and repeat the refresh recipe above. Repeat like this until you next need bread. 200g/7oz is enough to make 6 x 700g/1½lb loaves, with 50g/1¾oz starter left over to refresh and store.

Refresh timetable

Firstly, work out how much starter you want to use. For 3 x 700g/1½lb loaves you will need 75g/2¾oz, plus 25g/1oz of starter left over to refresh for the following week. It is likely that you will have too much starter.

Before setting out to make sourdough breads, many people worry about how the process (a minimum of 12 hours) will fit into their day. The following 'refresh' table is for sourdough baking on a Saturday morning.

Refresh 1 – Monday evening

Refresh 2 – Wednesday evening

Refresh 3 – Friday morning, ready to make dough on Friday afternoon

NB: ALWAYS REMEMBER TO KEEP SOME STARTER BACK FOR THE FOLLOWING WEEK'S BAKING!

If you bake 3 times a week, make enough for each session following the timetable above, and keep some back.

If you bake every day, you will have to keep a larger amount and refresh it daily as soon as each day's bread dough is made.

Tips and techniques

Your starter feeds on carbohydrate. It is best to keep the starter quite dry like a piece of dough and not in liquid form. In my experience too much moisture attracts rogue organisms that affect the taste of the bread and can ruin the starter.

Use the right flour. We have found that plain white organic flour keeps the starter in good health. Stone-milled white flour, which we use to make bread, tends to be a little oily. This is because when the grain is milled between stones, the oils are distributed through the flour. Modern 'roller-milling' techniques extract the oils from the flour. The high concentration of yeasts in the starter react to the oils in stone-milled flour by becoming overactive and fermenting very quickly. Unless you make bread every day, plain white flour is recommended. Italian '00' pasta flour also keeps the starter stable and is the best flour to use if you need to 'rescue' an over-fermented starter (see below).

The water needs to be fresh from the cold mains tap in the kitchen. Using water that has been in the hot-water tank risks contamination. Likewise boiled water and mineral water are unsuitable, although if you live in a place where the mains water is not for drinking, use ordinary bottled water. There is no real need to warm the water.

A few words about fermentation. Not being an expert on the subject, although an enthusiastic participant, I should still spell out the process: during fermentation, the yeasts contained in the starter feed on the carbohydrates (sugars) and produce alcohol and carbon dioxide, the gas that makes dough inflate and expand. Louis Pasteur, the first scientist to discover exactly which micro-organisms were involved in the process, made it beautifully clear for lay-bakers such as myself. Fermentation, he said, was 'respiration without air'.

When the starter is active, it will bubble and smell pleasant. If it begins to smell rancid and unpleasantly sour, it has over-fermented – the yeasts have run out of food (sugars) – and needs to be refreshed with more flour and water, and possibly more than once, before being used to make bread again. Do not try to make bread with over-fermented acidic starter otherwise it will taste unpleasant.

To refresh a starter that has over-fermented: Take a small amount from the base of the container, about 20g/¾oz, and refresh with 40g/1½oz water and 80g/3oz flour (we have found that Italian '00' flour is very effective when a starter needs rescuing, perhaps because it is a very dry, highly milled flour). Follow the usual refresh instructions (see page 32) then repeat twice before using to make bread, over a period of a week. Change the containers each time, and make sure they are properly cleaned and washed out with boiling water. After three times, the starter should smell healthy again.

Rye starter needs to be refreshed more often because, as with the stone-milled organic white bread flour, it becomes very active quickly. Put it in the fridge only 1–2 hours after refreshment to keep fermentation slow.

Throwing starter away. If you make bread once a week, beginning with 50g/1¾oz of starter, you will probably end up with too much on the second refresh. Before refresh 2, throw away or give away half the starter and weigh the remainder. Add its weight in water and twice its weight in flour. Eventually you will decide for yourself how much you are happy to work with. Of course it is always better to have too much than too little.

How much starter you need. The professional chart on page 39 shows how much starter you need for 1–24 loaves. Do not worry if you do not have enough, though. You can let the bread prove for longer, or put it in a warmer place than usual and it will soon develop and the ferment will happen.

THE FIRST BREAD – THE RECIPE

We really want you to make sourdough bread successfully from the start. Don't just read the recipe on the opposite page, make sure you have a good browse of the introduction to this chapter (pages 30–35).

This is the very first bread we made at the bakery, using bread expert Giuseppe Mascoli's instructions. He whizzed around to see us on his motorbike like a paramedic. My first attempt at making a sourdough starter had not gone well and he produced some of his own, which originated in Italy. The loaves I made that week were not a success, mainly because I burned the base of the bread – we were yet to use fireproof stone tiles in the oven.

On the second week, in spite of leaving the bread too long before baking so it was a little spread out and flat, it was delicious and our little following grew.

This is the basic recipe behind many in this part of the book and it can be adapted by referring to steps 1–5. You can also create breads of your own, substituting different flours and other ingredients.

I have tried to keep baker's jargon to a minimum but the most often repeated verb in bread-making, more than kneading, is 'proving'. To prove bread is to leave it in ideal conditions for the fermentation process, sometimes for hours. During this time the dough develops – it is the period where it gets its flavour and texture. I can't find a better term – 'leave to rise' seems rather mystical.

This recipe makes 3 x 700g/1½lb loaves. These loaves are free-standing. They are shaped into balls then wrapped in floured 'couche' cloths and positioned side by side in a box so their sides are supported as the dough rises. Alternatively, you can use baskets.

THE POCKET BAKERY WHITE SOURDOUGH

A simple recipe, ideal for beginners, which has four main stages of preparation then one stage of baking.

Stage 1. Mixing and kneading the dough

Stage 2. Folding the dough

Stage 3. Shaping the dough

Stage 4. Proving the bread before baking

Stage 5. Baking the bread

Quantities

The sourdough recipes in this chapter are for 3 x 700g/1½lb loaves (unless otherwise mentioned) because sourdough has good keeping qualities (often up to a week) and it is practical in families to have one bread-making day. But should you need to make just one loaf, or perhaps be enterprising and open your own small bakery, this chart gives quantities for making one 700g/1½lb loaf, and up to 24.

No. loaves	kg flour	litres water	grams sourdough starter	grams salt
1	0.5	0.33	25	10
3	1.5	1	75	30
6	3	2	150	60
9	4.5	3	225	90
15	7.5	5	375	150
24	12	8	600	240

Equipment

This is a basic list for traditional, artisan bread-making. For the recipes in this chapter, you may need the below equipment plus any other bits and pieces mentioned in the recipes themselves. Also see page 246 for suppliers.

- **Thermometer** that measures low temperatures – electronic thermometers are best.

- **Large shallow food container** that will take 7 litres/12 pints, preferably with a flat base and lid, or a large bowl with clingfilm to cover.

- **Container for liquid**, e.g. a jug.

- Food-safe disposable **gloves** (optional).

- 2 plastic **dough scrapers**.

- Stainless steel **dough cutter**, or sharp knife.

- **3 cloths** about 30x30cm/12x12 inches (cotton napkins are perfect) or 3 baskets, approximately 23cm/9 inches in diameter. Traditional proving baskets made from wood or wicker and other moulds can also be used. I also use the small wooden boxes that clementines are sometimes packed in.

- A round or rectangular **pizza stone** – loaves will have to be baked one at a time in a regular-size oven – or an untreated quarry tile no more than 2cm/½-inch thick.

- **Baker's peel**.

- One **razor blade** or baker's lame.

Timing

The process takes 16 hours, plus or minus, but don't worry, your input is minimal while proving is under way. If you begin this process at 2–3pm, it will be ready to fold at 5pm, then shape at 7pm ready to couche (a traditional French term for sleeping or overnight proving) until the morning, when it can be baked between 8 and 10am.

....

Storage

This bread keeps for about 6 days and is fine to use fresh for 3 days before toasting. Freshly baked loaves can be frozen when just cool and will taste as good as fresh when defrosted. Leftovers make rough breadcrumbs with a good strong savoury taste and can be frozen.

....

Ingredients

1kg/2lb 4oz **water**

70g/2½oz **sourdough starter**

30g/1 oz **salt**

1.5kg/3lb 5oz **strong white stoneground flour**

Approximately 500g/1lb 2oz **extra strong white flour** for dusting

Stage 1. Mixing and kneading the dough

Warm the water to 29°C, adding enough hot water from a kettle to cold tap water. Put the water in a large container and add the starter and salt. Mix with your hands so the starter begins to break apart. Put the flour in a large container or bowl, then add the water and starter mixture. Mix with your hands (I tend to use food-safe gloves for this stage because it is very messy) until you have a heavy, wet and lumpy dough that feels dry in places.

Turn the dough out on to the worktop. Clean out the container using the plastic dough scraper and set aside. Knead the dough on the worktop: stretch it away from you pushing with one hand while holding it near to you with the other hand. Then fold it, turn it around and repeat this action.

Ideally you want the dough to be quite sticky and tacky – a wet dough makes better bread. (But not so wet that you cannot pick it up with hands or dough scrapers.) If it feels too wet, add a small handful of flour.

Continue to knead – only add tiny amounts of flour if you feel it is still too wet. Every 3 minutes, pause for 3 minutes to allow the dough to relax. You will notice how it softens each time you do this. Once the dough is smooth, still sticky but easy to handle, pick it up and place in the container. The kneading process takes about 12–15 minutes. Cover with the lid and leave on the worktop for 2½ hours.

Stage 2. Folding the dough

The folding process strengthens the dough, meaning it ultimately makes loaves that sit high and do not spread all over the place even though the dough contains a lot of moisture. By now the dough will be beginning slowly to ferment. Carefully tip the dough out on to a lightly floured worktop. Lift one end (use dough scrapers; it is easier), stretching it a bit, and bring it over to fold – just as with a piece of cloth. Repeat 3 or 4 times from different ends of the dough, working north, east, south and west, then replace the dough in the container and cover. You could also use a large bowl and cover it with cling film if a container is not available.

Leave for a further 2–2½ hours.

Stage 3. Shaping the dough
Flour the cloths or baskets well. If you are nervous that the dough is very wet, be very generous with the flour. It does not matter if you use too much, but using too little will leave the shaped dough frustratingly stuck to the cloths or baskets.

Cut the dough into 3 pieces, approximately 800g/1lb 12oz each (the bread loses weight as it bakes). Lay one piece on the floured worktop, gently pressing out into a rectangle, then begin to roll it, pressing firmly in the centre at intervals with all your fingers. This forms a core at the centre of the loaf, giving it strength.

Now use one hand to cup the end of the roll and curve it round underneath. Repeat this action until you have a smooth ball. Place it, the smoothest side down (this will be the top crust of the bread once baked) on the dusted cloth or in the basket. Repeat.

If you used cloths, place all 3 loaves, snuggled side by side, in a box or back in the (cleaned) container, or in anything where they can sit supported. It is important to shape and 'couche' the loaves quickly so they do not relax and lose their shape.

Stage 4. Proving the bread before baking
Ideally bread should be proved in a humid atmosphere. If covered, it will create its own moisture as it 'breathes'. Cover the container with foil, making sure the foil cannot touch the rising bread, and place in a cool area at about 15°C. This could be in the garden protected from animals or rain. We put ours in a box with a fitted lid and a refuse bag secured with elastic. You can also place it in a shed, or if it is winter and cold, in an unheated room. Use a weather thermometer to check the temperature, but in time you will be able to judge this (see The Mind of a Baker, page 25).

Leave overnight or for 14 hours. The bread will nearly double in size, yet feel firm and cool.

Stage 5. Baking the bread
Preheat the oven to 220°C/425°F/Gas mark 7, placing the baking stone(s) inside the oven before turning it on (this will make it take longer to heat than usual).

Place a baker's peel (paddle-shaped tool) on the worktop and flour it well. Tip one loaf gently on to the peel to reveal the underside – now the surface of the loaf – then use a razor-sharp blade to make a single, 1cm-deep score across the whole surface. You can make a cross, more than one cut or even a pattern, but on the first attempt score the loaf once, then immediately pick up the peel and slide the bread on to the stone.

Bake for 5 minutes then, without opening the oven door, turn the heat down to 200°C/400°F/Gas mark 6. Bake for 25–35 minutes, until the bread is a deep tanned brown. The bread should burst handsomely in the centre, raising the height. Cool the bread on a rack. Depending on the oven you use, the crust will soften slightly as it cools. For a thicker, darker crust, continue to cook for a further 10 minutes.

Cut the bread when cool or slightly warm – the texture inside can collapse if the bread is too hot.

Tips and techniques

- If the bread is hard, dry and cakey, the dough was too dry and did not prove for long enough. Add more water to the dough in the early kneading part, stage 1. The perfect dough feels sticky to the touch.

- If the bread spreads out in the oven during baking, the dough is over-proved due to being kept in too warm an atmosphere or for too long. If it is summer and difficult to keep the loaves cool as they prove, shorten the proving time by 4 hours, starting the process later in the day and shaping late at night. Alternatively, use just a quarter of the starter quantity to slow down the ferment.

- If the bread has a curved base and does not open out during cooking, appearing 'tight' and the interior is cakey, the dough is a little dry or under-proved. Add more water next time, and make sure to score a large enough cut with the blade. Also it may have dried out after shaping – the shaped bread must be covered unless left to rise in a humid atmosphere. Use foil loosely draped over the loaves (you can reuse it every time you bake).

- If the bread bursts open at the sides, it is under-proved or may need to be scored a little more.

- The loaf takes ages to cook – stop opening the oven door to check it! You are letting all the heat out.

RAISIN BREAD

An unsweetened bread that was immediately popular with our first customers. Parents reported back that children who had never wanted anything but soft white bread were devouring heaps of it toasted for breakfast.

Use organic raisins for this bread because they do not contain sulphites, a preservative that can interfere with the living yeasts in the sourdough, slowing the development of the dough and making the bread heavy. You can add non-organic raisins to a bread made with commercial yeast as it is much more active. Refer to the five stages on pages 39–41 before you begin making this bread.

Makes 3 x 800g/1lb 12oz loaves

Equipment
As for White Sourdough (page 39)

Timing
As for White Sourdough (page 40)

Storage
This loaf keeps for 6–7 days. When it is dry and in its 'twilight', you can cut it into thin slices and bake until crisp. Store in an airtight container.

Ingredients
1kg/2lb 4oz water
70g/2 ½oz sourdough starter
30g/1oz salt
1.5kg/3lb 5oz strong white stoneground flour
450g/1lb organic raisins
Approximately 500g/1lb 2oz extra strong white flour for dusting

Mixing, kneading and folding the dough

Warm the water to 29°C, adding enough hot water from a kettle to cold tap water. Put the water in a large jug or container and add the starter and salt. Mix with your hands so the starter begins to break apart. Put the flour and raisins in the large container or bowl, then add the water and starter mixture. Mix with your hands (I tend to use food-safe gloves for this stage because it is very messy) until you have a heavy, wet and lumpy dough that feels dry in places. Continue as on pages 40–41 to the end of stage 2.

Shaping the bread

Flour the cloths or baskets well. If you are nervous that the dough is very wet, be very generous with the flour. It does not matter if you use too much but using too little will leave the shaped dough frustratingly stuck to the cloths or baskets.

Cut the dough into 3 pieces, approximately 975g/2lb 3oz each (the bread loses weight as it bakes). Lay one piece on the floured worktop, gently pressing out into a rectangle then roll it like a loose Swiss roll.

Place each roll upside down on a floured cloth and fit into a container that holds the 3 snugly so they support each other as the bread rises, or, if you are using baskets, place each roll in a floured basket.

Follow stage 4 on page 41 to prove the bread.

Preheat the oven to 220°C/425°F/Gas mark 7, placing baking stone(s) inside the oven before turning it on. Place a baker's peel on the worktop and flour it well. Tip one loaf gently on to the peel to reveal the underside – now the surface of the loaf – then use a razor-sharp blade to make a single, 1cm-deep score about 12cm/4½ inches across. Immediately pick up the peel and slide the bread on to the stone.

Bake for 5 minutes then, without opening the oven door, turn the heat down to 200°C/400°F/Gas mark 6. Bake for 25–35 minutes, until the bread is a deep tanned brown. Cool the bread on a rack.

RYE BREAD

Weighty like bullion with the flavour of a thousand nut groves and a biscuit crust, rye bread is the grail for many artisan bread enthusiasts. The flour contains very little gluten, which is a bonus for people who are intolerant to glutinous bread, but something of a headache for the baker. Without much gluten and with the grain reacting quickly on contact with the starter/ yeast, it can easily over-prove and the little gas that develops within a loaf can deflate. Adding a higher-gluten wheat flour defeats the purpose, but we found another carbohydrate to help make the bread lighter – grated cooked potato. We also add a little fresh commercial yeast to rye bread to help keep it airy.

Timing is all with this bread, and temperature is important. This bread has one extra stage, best done approximately 6 hours or the night before you mix the main dough. Unlike the white bread, rye needs a shorter time proving with a higher temperature. The baker's art is to 'catch' it before it collapses.

Makes 3 x 750g/1lb 10oz loaves

Equipment

As for White Sourdough
(page 39), plus:
3 x 900g/2lb **loaf tins** and baking
parchment to line them

Timing

Total 14 hours

Storage

Keeps for 2–3 days. It will become
very dense after 2 days.

Mixing the starter ferment

Mix the starter, rye flour and water together in a bowl until you have a smooth paste. Cover with cling film and leave to prove for 6 hours or overnight at room temperature.

Mixing the main dough

Warm the 750g/1lb 10oz water to 29°C. Put the water in a container or jug and add the starter ferment (above), molasses and salt. Mix with your hands so the starter begins to break apart. Add the potatoes and yeast, and mix. Put the flour, rye grains and seeds in the large container or bowl and add the water/starter/potato and mix with your hands using food-safe gloves. Rye dough is rather like stirring mud – it will not make a smooth dough, but a thick paste.

Ideally you want the dough to be smooth and wet but pliable like pastry dough. Pinch it with your fingers – if it cracks, add more water, but not too much as rye bread will not cook if the dough is the wrong consistency. Once the dough is well mixed (this takes about 5 minutes), shape it straight away.

Shaping the bread

Cut the dough into 3 x 850g/2lb pieces. Press them out with your hands into a rectangular shape then fold in half once and smooth the surface of the loaf using wet hands. Roll the loaf in flour then place it, smooth side up, on a sheet of baking parchment. Wrap the sheet up the sides of the loaf and drop it into the tin. Sprinkle over a little flour. You do not need to score this bread. During proving the surface of the loaf cracks like scorched earth, very much a characteristic of a pure rye bread.

Cover the tins loosely with foil, place in a warm, draught-free spot – about 25–29°C (an airing cupboard is perfect). Leave for 6–8 hours. The bread is ready to bake when the loaves have nearly doubled in size and the surface is covered in cracks about ½cm/¼ inch wide.

Baking the bread

Preheat the oven to 220°C/425°F/Gas mark 7. Place the tins in the oven; bake for 5 minutes then turn down the heat to 200°C/400°F/Gas mark 6 and bake for 35–45 minutes. For the last 10 minutes, take the bread out of the tins and paper and return to the oven to crisp the sides.

Place on a rack until completely cool, then wrap in foil or a plastic bag to keep the bread fresh.

Tips and techniques

- Rye flour is very variable – if at first you have problems, tweak the moisture and proving time until you find the right conditions. It is well worth persevering with this recipe, we promise! Keep a pencil to hand, and scribble your records by this recipe.

- If the bread is undercooked inside, you need to shorten the proving time by an hour or more.

- If the bread surface breaks wide open, it has not been proved long enough.

- Increase the water content slightly if the bread is too heavy.

- Make sure the potatoes are not overcooked. If they become mushy they will not help lighten the dough.

Ingredients

For the first stage – the starter ferment:

70g/2½oz sourdough starter, either rye-based or white-flour-based starter*

250g/9oz organic light rye flour

250g/9oz water

For the main dough:

750g/1lb 10oz water

115g/4oz molasses

30g/1oz salt

2–3 medium-sized potatoes, boiled whole, skinned and grated

28g/1oz fresh yeast

1.25kg/2lb 12oz organic light rye flour

100g/3½oz whole rye grains or kibbled (cracked) rye grains

100g/3½oz sunflower seeds

100g/3½oz green pumpkin seeds

Approximately 500g/1lb 2oz extra rye flour for dusting

* Rye starter care: A rye starter must be cared for in a similar way to white, but refreshed more often and only left out to become active for 2 hours before being stored in the fridge. Refresh every 2 days.

Uncooked

Cooked

WHOLEMEAL SPELT & HONEY BREAD

Spelt is an ancient grain, dating back thousands of years and used long before the development of modern wheat plants. Like rye flour it reacts quickly to the yeasts in the sourdough so usually needs less proving time overall. When kneading it we notice that, unlike other wholemeal flours, it has an extraordinary silky texture, as if the ferment can't wait to happen. It contains less gluten than modern wheat flours, which means it can over-prove and compact in on itself.

Makes 3 loaves, each weighing about 750–800g/1lb 10–12oz

....

Equipment

As for White Sourdough (page 39)

....

Timing

Make this bread later in the day, beginning in the early evening to bake the next morning. Or start in the morning to bake in the early evening.

....

Storage

This bread keeps well for up to 5 days.

....

Ingredients

1kg/2lb 4oz water

2 tablespoons clear honey

70g/2½oz sourdough starter

30g/1oz salt

1.5kg/3lb 5oz stoneground spelt flour

Approximately 500g/1lb 2oz extra spelt flour for dusting

2 tablespoons cracked wheat or wholemeal flour

Mixing and kneading the dough

Warm the water to 29°C. Put it in a container or jug and add the honey, starter and salt. Mix with your hands so the starter begins to break apart. Put the flour in a large container or bowl and continue to mix with your hands (using food-safe gloves) until you have a wet and lumpy dough.

Turn the dough out on to the worktop. Clean out the container using the plastic dough scraper and set aside. Knead the dough on the worktop: stretch it away from you pushing with one hand while holding it near to you with the other hand. Then fold it, turn it around and repeat this kneading action.

Continue to knead – only add tiny amounts of flour if you feel it is still too wet. Every 3 minutes, pause for 3 minutes to allow the dough to relax. You will notice how it softens each time you do this. Once the dough is smooth, still sticky but easy to handle, pick it up and place in the container. The kneading process takes about 10 minutes. Cover with the lid and leave on the worktop for 2½ hours.

Folding the dough

This process strengthens the dough. By now the dough will be beginning slowly to ferment. Carefully tip the dough out on to a lightly floured worktop. Lift one end and bring it over to fold – just as with a piece of cloth. Repeat 3 or 4 times from different ends of the dough, working north, east, south and west, then replace the dough in the container and cover.

Place in a cooler place now, about 15°C, to slow the process of the fermentation. Leave for a further 1½ hours.

Shaping the dough

Flour the cloths or baskets well. If you are nervous that the dough is very wet, be very generous with the flour. Cut the dough into 3 pieces, approximately 850g/1lb 14oz each (the bread loses weight as it bakes). Lay one piece on the floured worktop, gently pressing out into a triangle, then roll it like a loose croissant.

Place each loaf in a floured cloth and put each into a loaf tin.

Proving the bread before baking

Ideally bread should be proved in a humid atmosphere. If covered, it will create its own moisture as it 'breathes'. Cover the tins with foil, making sure the foil cannot touch the rising bread, and place in a cool area at about 15°C. This could be in the garden protected from animals or rain. We put ours in a box with a fitted lid and a refuse bag secured with elastic. You can also place it in a shed, or if it is winter and cold, in an unheated room in your home. Use a weather thermometer to check the temperature but in time you will be able to judge this (see The Mind of a Baker, page 25).

Leave for 6–8 hours; the bread will nearly double in size, yet feel firm and cool.

Baking the bread

Preheat the oven to 240°C/475°F/Gas mark 9, placing baking stone(s) inside.

Place a baker's peel on the worktop and flour it well. Immediately pick up the peel and slide the bread on to the stone. Brush the surface with a little water and sprinkle over the cracked wheat or wholemeal flour.

Bake for 5 minutes then, without opening the oven door, turn the heat down to 220°C/425°F/Gas mark 7. Bake for 20–30 minutes, until the bread is a deep tanned brown. The bread should burst handsomely in the centre, raising the height. To test if done, tap it on the underside – it should sound hollow. Cool the bread on a rack. For a thicker crust, turn the oven down to 200°C/400°F/Gas mark 6 and bake for about 40 minutes. Leave to cool on a rack.

MALTED BROWN BREAD 'TIN'

No better bread exists for a proper egg and watercress sandwich, and made with a sourdough it puts all soft, sliced and wrapped 'granary bread' to shame. It is still toothsome enough though, for children to enjoy, and chewing on the crust is part of its beauty. To maximise the crust, choose tins that are long and slim, to make attractive little sandwiches for picnics.

Makes 3 x 700g/1 ½lb loaves

Equipment

As for White Sourdough (page 39), plus:

3 loaf tins, approximately 1kg/2lb capacity, greased with oil

Timing

The extra sugars in this dough, from the malt, will activate the energy in the bread and it will rise faster than a white loaf. Make it in the morning to bake in the afternoon – just in time for tea.

Ingredients

1kg/2lb 4oz water

70g/2½oz sourdough starter

70g/2½oz barley malt

30g/1oz salt

1.5kg/3lb 5oz Maltstar or granary flour

To glaze:

1 tablespoon malt mixed with 1 tablespoon milk

Mixing and kneading the dough

Warm the water to 29°C. Put in a container or jug and add the starter, malt and salt. Mix with your hands so the starter begins to break apart. Put the flour in the large container and pour in the water/starter mixture. Mix with your hands (I tend to use food-safe gloves for the mixing stage because it is very messy) until you have a wet and lumpy dough.

Turn the dough out on to the worktop, cleaning out the container with a scraper. Knead on the worktop: stretching, folding and pulling the dough. Ideally you want the dough to be quite sticky and tacky – a wet dough makes better bread – but not so wet that you cannot pick it up with hands or dough scrapers. If it feels too wet, add a small handful of flour.

Continue to knead – only add tiny amounts of flour if you feel it is still too wet. Every 3 minutes, pause for 3 minutes to allow the dough to relax. You will notice how it softens each time you do this. Once the dough is smooth, still sticky but easy to handle, pick it up and place in the container. The kneading process takes about 12–15 minutes. Cover with the lid and leave to prove for 1 hour.

Folding the dough

By now the dough will begin slowly to ferment. Carefully tip the dough out on to a lightly floured worktop. Lift one end and bring it over to fold – just as with a piece of cloth. Repeat 3 or 4 times from different ends of the dough, working north, east, south and west, then replace the dough in the container and cover.

Put in a cooler place now, about 15°C, to slow the process of the fermentation. Leave for a further hour before shaping.

Shaping the dough

Cut the dough into 3 pieces, approximately 800g/1lb 12oz each (the bread loses weight as it bakes). Lay one piece on the floured worktop, gently pressing out into a square, then roll it like a loose Swiss roll. Neaten the ends of the roll and place smooth side up in the tins.

Proving the bread before baking

Cover loosely with foil (so the dough does not come in contact with it) and place in a warm draught-free area. The bread will prove quite fast this way, in approximately 5 hours.

Baking the bread

Preheat the oven to 220°C/425°F/Gas mark 7.

Brush the surface of the swollen loaves with the malt/milk glaze. Use a razor-sharp blade to make a few diagonal scores on the surface, approximately ½cm/¼ inch, then place in the oven.

Bake for 5 minutes then, without opening the oven door, turn the heat down to 200°C/400°F/Gas mark 6. Bake for 20–30 minutes until well risen and a lovely glossy brown. For crisper sides, remove the bread from the tin and return to the oven 5 minutes before the end of the cooking time.

Leave to cool on a rack before slicing.

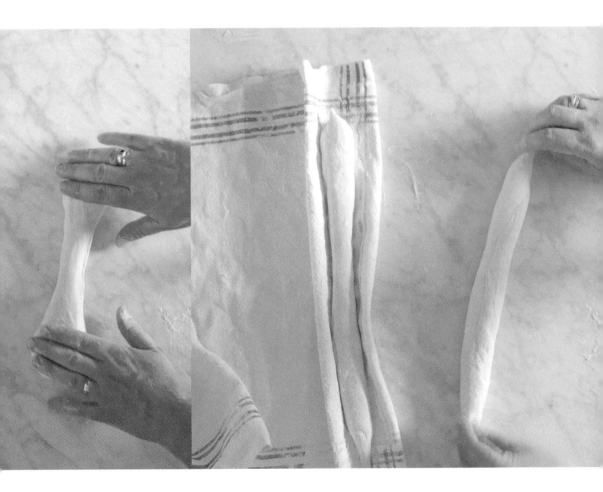

WHITE SOURDOUGH SPEARS

Our Pocket Bakery spears are not really baguettes, being too small and not made with French flour, but they have a lot of character and fans like their sturdiness and – when we get them right – the lovely large holes inside the bread. Their name comes from the sharp point at each end. If the crust is good, there is something sharp and menacing about them.

Shaping the dough

Flour the cloth well and place it on a tray or board, pleated to accommodate the 5 spear-shaped breads – the grooves in the pleats need to be wide and deep enough for the spears (about 7cm/2½ inches). If you are nervous that the dough is very wet, be very generous with the flour. It does not matter if you use too much, but using too little will leave the dough frustratingly stuck to the cloth.

Cut the dough into 5 long pieces, approximately 300g each. Lay the pieces on a floured board, stretching them to 50cm/20 inches max (or whatever length can be accommodated by the depth of your oven).

Lay one piece on the floured worktop and gently press out into a rectangle. Fold 3cm/1 inch of the short ends of the strip inwards and press them down. Now roll the length of the spear, pressing down with your fingers firmly at intervals, then roll using the flat of your hands into a long, slim, sausage shape. Pull and twist the ends to make points like a spear. Quickly lift it and place in a groove of the pleated cloth. Sprinkle a little more flour over it.

Repeat this process 4 more times. There should be enough for 5 breads. Cover the tray loosely with aluminium foil and place in a cool area (15°C). Leave to prove for about 11 hours (overnight).

Baking the bread

Preheat the oven to 240°C/475°F/Gas mark 9, placing baking stone(s) inside it.

Place a baker's peel on the worktop and flour it well. Tip one loaf gently on to the peel to reveal the underside, then use a razor-sharp blade to make a series of long (10cm/4-inch) cuts at an angle along the length of the spear. Immediately pick up the peel and slide the bread on to the stone.

Bake for 5 minutes, then, without opening the oven door, turn the heat down to 220°C/425°F/Gas mark 7. Bake for 15–20 minutes, until the bread is a golden brown and 'opening out' through the slits in the sticks. Lift out with the peel and cool. Eat as soon as you want; hot or cool.

Makes 5 spears, each weighing about 270–300g/10oz

Equipment

As for the White Sourdough on page 39, but in place of the couche cloths or baskets, you will need a 1-metre-long, 60cm-wide (3 feet x 2 feet) strip of thick textured cotton or linen for moulding the loaves, or 2 rough cotton/linen tea cloths. You can buy specially shaped metal baguette trays, but still line them with floured cloth, which makes it extra easy to space the spears and support their shape.

You will also need a longer peel (with a 60cm x 20cm paddle) to pick up the bread, though we have managed by holding the peel with an extra spatula to support the length of the loaf.

Timing

This is a slow-fermentation bread. Begin the first stage in the early afternoon and shape in the early evening. The breads prove overnight in a very cool place, for baking early morning.

Storage

This bread keeps well for a day and can be used for toasting over the next 2 days if stored in a plastic bag. Make a beautiful toasted 'tartine' (half a spear, cut lengthways) to eat buttered with scrambled eggs for breakfast.

Ingredients

1 quantity of White Sourdough (pages 40–41), prepared to the end of stage 3

Approximately 500g/1lb strong white flour for dusting

BREADS MADE WITH SPONGE FERMENTS

Professional bakers often start breads with either a 'poolish' or a 'sponge ferment', which serves the dual purpose of speeding up the process when there is little yeast, and developing the dough to improve taste and texture. A sponge is a batter-type mix, always quite wet, that is made with a proportion of the flour, yeast or starter, and water. The lack of salt and high liquid content in the mixture means that the ferment is quick. In the second stage, when the remaining flour, salt and water go in, more starter is added to make the dough very active, quickly. While I love the texture of our original sourdough and the simplicity of the five-stage process, these breads made with sponge ferments do have lots of character and a great appearance.

MARY BREAD

This is named after my grandmother, but ring-shaped bread is also often made on feast days in Europe, and the sight of them is instantly festive and suggests large gatherings. Putting a few breads on the table and allowing guests or family to tear them creates a friendly air.

Another lovely way to serve Mary bread is to split it horizontally into two rings and briefly grill them rubbed with fresh tomato and garlic before dribbling over olive oil and scattering with oregano leaves. Totally guaranteed to please.

This dough is based on low-profile, open-textured Italian breads, and is made very slowly with an ordinary plain white flour. It is a wet-textured dough with little strength and will spread, so you have to be cautious to mould it into a thin shape or the ring will just bleed into a disc.

This bread combines the use of fresh commercial yeast and sourdough, starting with a fermented sponge. The process is lengthy, though not hard work, which is why it is good for high days and holidays when more people are at home.

Mary bread is literally the grandmother of bread recipes; a greater family of breads can be made following this method. Following this recipe are variations but also use it to create your own.

Makes 2 x 24cm rings,
weighing about 250g/9oz each

....

Equipment

As for White Sourdough (page 39) but no cloths or baking stones are needed – only 2 **baking sheets**, either oiled then dusted with flour, or lined with baking parchment and dusted with flour.

....

Timing

The original ferment takes 16 hours – make it in the early evening for use the next morning. The remaining process takes 2¾–3¼ hours to complete.

....

Storage

Eat on the day or toasted the next day. This bread freezes very well if frozen when freshly baked, and leftovers make great bread soups with tomato, stock, beans and garlic, or big flaky breadcrumbs to toast and add to Caesar salads.

....

Ingredients

For the sponge ferment:

3g/½ teaspoon **fresh yeast** or 2g dried yeast

150g/5½oz **water**

100g/3½oz **strong white flour**

50g/1¾oz **wholemeal flour**

For the dough:

1 quantity **sponge ferment** (above)

50g/1¼oz **White Sourdough starter** (page 30)

180g/6½oz **Italian '00' white flour**

15g/1 tablespoon **extra virgin olive oil**

5g **sea salt**

85g/3oz **water**, or more

The day before

Mix the sponge ferment ingredients well and leave to ferment in a plastic container with a lid at room temperature for 16 hours.

. . . .

Stage 1. Mixing and kneading the dough

Put the ferment in a large flat-bottomed container or a bowl with the rest of the dough ingredients and mix with a spoon or your hands to a wet dough. Knead vigorously – you can use wet dough scrapers if you find the dough too sticky to handle. Scoop and fold the dough over on itself, pausing every 3 minutes to give the dough a rest when it becomes tight. Continue like this for about 15 minutes. This stage can be done in a mixer fitted with a dough hook in about 7 minutes; just turn it off occasionally to allow the resting periods.

Leave the dough to prove for 1 hour, at room temperature, covered.

Stage 2. Folding the dough

Fold the dough using wet dough scrapers – picking it up gently at one edge so as not to disturb the bubbles, then bringing it into the centre. Do this from all sides until you have a higher mound of dough. Leave to prove for a further 30 minutes.

Stage 3. Shaping the dough

Dust the worktop with a generous amount of flour and gently tip the dough on to the surface, again being careful not to deflate it too much.

Dip the dough scraper in more flour then press it down the centre of the dough to cut it in half and divide it. Sprinkle flour over the surface, then pick up one piece and stretch to a long slim strip about 45cm/18 inches long. If the dough tightens, pause before stretching it to the length you want.

Lift the dough on to the baking sheet and form it into a ring, pinching the ends (dampen with a little water) gently together. If it looks a mess you can tidy it a little, tucking it in – mind those bubbles! – once it has sat on the sheet for a minute or two.

Do the same with the second piece of dough.

Stage 4. Proving the dough

Leave the rings to prove for 1–2 hours – they need to be very bubbly; it does not matter if they look a little flat.

Stage 5. Baking the bread

After 1 hour, preheat the oven to 220°C/425°F/ Gas mark 7. The loaves are ready to bake when the dough has risen as much as it can without the bubbles beginning to burst. Bake for about 15 minutes. It is ready when pale brown and crisp. It will soften as it cools on the rack.

. . . .

Variations

- Now and then it is nice to serve a warm loaf, straight from the oven, and Mary dough is ideal. This soft, wide-open-textured dough is very versatile and practical to make once the sponge is fermented because the final stages can be prepared before lunch or between 6pm and dinner.

- Use the basic Mary bread recipe to make soft yet chewy rolls to fill with lunchtime things, or simple flat breads to serve with big stews and soups. Use the dough scraper or a sharp knife to sever pieces from the dough and transfer them carefully to baking sheets just as they are without changing the shapes, preserving the air bubbles inside them. Bake for 10–12 minutes at 220°C/425°F/ Gas mark 7.

SWEET TEA BREAD

Sticky slices of fruity bread, made all the better with a sour-dough base. This improves the keeping quality of the bread – over a week – and makes a light yet strong-textured crumb. Make with untreated, organically produced dried fruit (i.e. preservative-free) if possible, as it interferes less with the yeasts in the sourdough, keeping it active.

Put the tea in a bowl, add all the fruit and leave to soak for 30 minutes, then drain and discard excess tea. If you do not soak the fruit it can absorb moisture in the bread and make a dry loaf.

Put the lukewarm milk in a bowl and add the starter, yeast and 1 teaspoon of the sugar. Whisk to dissolve the yeast and set aside for 15 minutes. Small bubbles will likely form on the surface. Add the rest of the sugar, the melted butter, eggs and vanilla, then stir well to combine.

Put the flour in a large bowl and add the salt, fruit and spices. Stir a few times then add the milk and yeast mixture. Mix to a soft, sticky, heavy dough. If it is dry add a little cold water. Remove the dough from the bowl using dough scrapers and knead briefly, for about 3 minutes. Place back in the bowl, cover with cling film and leave to prove for 1 hour.

After 1 hour, tip the dough out on to the worktop and fold it, picking up one edge, stretching it out then up and over. Repeat from the other edge, and again on each side, one more. The dough should feel tight. Replace back in the bowl, cover with cling film and leave to prove for 30 minutes.

To shape the bread, press it into a rectangle about 20cm/8 inches wide, then roll it into a loose sausage. Smooth the ends of the roll and place in the prepared tin.

Leave to prove for about 3–4 hours, until well risen and aerated. Do not let it get too high and wobbly or the dough will over-prove and the bread will lose height during baking.

To bake, preheat the oven to 200°C/400°F/Gas mark 6. Brush the loaf with the beaten egg and place the tin in the oven. Turn down the heat after 5 minutes to 190°C/375°F/Gas mark 5 and bake for about 40–50 minutes. If the loaf looks as if it might burn, turn the oven down by 10°C.

Makes 1 loaf, about 1.25kg/2lb 12oz

Equipment

20–25cm/8–10 inch long loaf tin, lined with baking parchment

Timing

A slow bread that will take longer to prove; make in the morning to eat for tea.

Storage

Keeps for a week; good to eat fresh for 4 days and makes good toast thereafter. Freeze for up to a month.

Ingredients

200ml/7fl oz brewed Earl Grey tea

50g/2oz organic currants

50g/2oz organic sultanas

225g/8oz organic pitted prunes, halved

125ml/4½fl oz lukewarm milk

100g/3½oz white or rye sourdough starter

3g/¼ teaspoon dried yeast or 7g/¼oz fresh yeast

6 tablespoons light soft brown sugar

110g/4oz butter, melted and cooled, plus extra for greasing

2 eggs, lightly beaten

½ teaspoon vanilla extract

450g/1lb strong white flour, sifted, plus extra for dusting

½ teaspoon salt

1 heaped teaspoon ground cinnamon

1 heaped teaspoon ground allspice

1 egg, beaten

BLACK GRAPE BREAD

Many years ago I ate a bread like this that had been made to celebrate the harvest on a vineyard – it is the splash of aniseed liquor that makes it so special. Make it with sweet Muscat grapes if you can find them.

Makes 2 small loaves,
about 250g/9oz each

Equipment

As for White Sourdough
(page 39) but no cloths or baking
stones are needed –
only 2 baking sheets

Timing

As for Mary Bread, the original
ferment takes 16 hours – make it in
the early evening for use the next
morning. The remaining process
takes 2¾–3¼ hours to complete.

Storage

Eat on the day or store for 2 days.

Ingredients

1 quantity Mary Bread dough
(pages 63–64) prepared to the
end of stage 2

400g/14oz sweet ripe grapes,
seeds removed (if not
already seedless)

2 tablespoons aniseed liqueur
(e.g. Pernod)

4 tablespoons caster sugar

Dust the worktop with a generous amount of flour and gently tip the dough on to the surface, being careful not to deflate it.

Dip the dough scraper in more flour then press it down the centre of the dough to cut it in half and divide it. Sprinkle flour over the surface, then pick up one piece and stretch to about 30cm/12 inches long and 25cm/10 inches wide. If the dough tightens, pause before stretching it to the length you want.

Quickly scatter a third of the grapes over the surface, followed by one tablespoon of the aniseed liqueur and half the sugar. Fold the dough in half and lift on to the baking sheet. Dampen the edges a little with fingers dipped into water to seal. The most important thing is not to disturb the activity of the gas in the dough – or as little as possible.

Repeat with the other half of the dough, placing on the second baking sheet. Scatter the remaining grapes over the surface of both loaves, letting them fall at will. Leave to prove for 45 minutes. Preheat the oven to 200°C/400°F/Gas mark 6 then bake for 25–30 minutes or until puffed and crisp – the juice from the cooked grapes will bleed a little.

Eat while still warm from the oven – with a glass of sweet wine.

FIG & PUMPKIN BREAD

This is a sweet-savoury seasonal bread to have with those first creamy cold weather soups, along with hunks of mature Cheddar cheese. It was inspired by a bread made in an Italian bakery, eaten at Halloween.

Makes 2 small loaves, about
250g/9oz each

. . . .

Equipment

As for White Sourdough
(page 39) but no cloths or baking
stones are needed –
only 2 **baking sheets**

. . . .

Timing

As for Mary Bread, the original
ferment takes 16 hours – make it in
the early evening for use the next
morning. The remaining process
takes 2¾–3¼ hours to complete.

. . . .

Storage

As for Mary Bread, but do not
freeze for more than a month to
prevent the fruit drying out.

. . . .

Ingredients

1 quantity **Mary Bread dough**
(pages 63–64) prepared to the
end of stage 2

300g/10½oz **pumpkin,**
roughly grated

6 **fresh figs**
or 6 dried soft figs, sliced

Dust the worktop with a generous amount of flour and gently tip the dough on to the surface, being careful not to deflate it.

Dip the dough scraper in more flour then press it down the centre of the dough to cut it in half and divide it. Sprinkle flour over the surface of one piece, then gently press it out into a rectangle about the size of an A4 sheet of paper. Scatter over half the pumpkin and figs then, with floured hands, fold the bread in half. Press it down again with your fingers, and fold again to work the pumpkin and figs carefully into the dough. Do this again with the second piece of dough. Lift the loaves on to the baking sheet, and leave to prove for 1–2 hours.

After an hour, preheat the oven to 220°C/425°F/Gas mark 7. The loaves are ready to bake when the dough has risen to a peak, as much as it can, but is not becoming soft and collapsing. Bake for about 15 minutes. It is ready when golden and crisp. It will soften as it cools on the rack.

Variations
Roasted cherry tomato and oregano; baked winter rhubarb; sweet onions and crispy pork; stinging nettles; wild garlic; cobnut and sloe.

OPEN SANDWICH BREAD

Ever since visiting Denmark I have loved these dense, wet breads that invite great heaps of smoked fish, dressing and cress to be piled over thin slices. They never inflate much, and are best made the day before eating to allow them to become juicier and hold together.

This bread is made with a preliminary 'sponge' – which gives the dough a chance to get going on the ferment before all the heavy seeds and wholegrains are added.

First make the sponge. Mix together the sponge ingredients to a smooth batter and leave covered with cling film in a warm place (preferably 30°C – I put mine on top of the water boiler in the bathroom) for 2–3 hours. You will see a slight swelling in the mixture and the odd bubble.

For the main dough, put the rye flour, potato, yeast, kibbled rye and seeds in a large bowl or stand mixer, add the rest of the ingredients and the sponge, and mix. The dough should be sludgy and slightly sticky. If the dough feels very dry (this may be due to the flour variety), add a little more water. Roll it into a log on a floured surface. Put the dough into the lined tin. Brush the surface of the loaf with water and scatter more rye flour, rye flakes or sunflower and pumpkin seeds on top.

Leave to rise for about 5–6 hours, covered lightly with foil, until the loaf has increased in size by one-third to one-half. Preheat the oven to 200°C/400°F/Gas mark 6. Put in the oven and turn the heat down to 180°C/350°F/Gas mark 4 as soon as the door is closed. Bake for 35–45 minutes – the loaf should smell nutty, feel lighter, and be golden brown. Remove from the tin, take off the baking paper and put the loaf back in the oven for 3–5 minutes.

Allow to cool completely, then wrap in aluminium foil for at least 4 hours, or ideally overnight, before slicing.

Variation
Add 2 teaspoons of caraway seeds to the dough along with the other seeds, and scatter a few more on top before baking for bread that is outstanding with smoked pastrami, smoked cheese or roast beef.

Makes 1 loaf weighing about 800g/1lb 12oz

Equipment

As for White Sourdough (page 39), plus:

20–22cm/8–9-inch **loaf tin** and baking parchment to line them

Timing

Make this dough in the morning to bake later in the afternoon. If you have a warm spot, about 30°C, for proving, it will speed up the process.

Storage

Ideally, make the bread the day before use, then wrap in foil once cool; it keeps for 6 days.

Ingredients

For the 'sponge':

150ml/¼ pint lukewarm **water**

30g/1oz **sourdough rye starter**

150g/5½oz **light rye flour**

1 tablespoon organic **molasses**

For the main dough:

350g/12oz **light rye flour**

1 medium-sized **potato**, boiled whole, skinned and grated

10g/¼ oz **yeast**

50g/1¾oz **kibbled rye** or flakes

50g/1¾oz **sunflower seeds**

50g/1¾oz **green pumpkin seeds**

2 tablespoons organic **molasses**

10g/¼oz **salt**

175ml/6fl oz lukewarm **water**

To finish:

Extra **rye flour**, plus **kibbled rye** or rye flakes, sunflower and pumpkin seeds

Modern
bread

We call these breads modern, or new, yet they are made with yeast that has been in use for over 150 years. But when you compare these breads to sourdoughs, which are believed to have been used in Ancient Egyptian baking, the 'commercial' yeast we can now buy in shops is an infant. The difference between the two simply is that while sourdough contains slow-acting, often mysterious micro-life, we know about the active contents of commercial yeast.

Modern yeast is fast acting and entirely predictable so is a good starting point for new bakers who want quick results. Sourdoughs and modern breads have other differences, however. New breads keep for less time and, because the fermentation is fast, other ingredients like fat and sugar sometimes need to be added to help with the texture and flavour elements that come naturally with slow-fermented, traditional breads. Adding fat enhances the flavour, for example, and sugar is added to change the appearance of the crumb.

For me, commercial yeast lends itself best to the kind of breads you want to eat almost straight from the oven: whiter, softer breads cooked in tins or gorgeously soft, sweet and rich buns that somehow do not lend themselves to sourdough so well.

The yeast itself is grown on malt and comes in either fresh form, dried granules or in very small grains usually called 'easy-bake' or 'quick', which can be added straight to the flour and do not need to be activated with liquid first to dissolve the yeast. The granules are small enough to be dispersed throughout the flour, and dissolve quickly once the liquid is added. The recipes in this chapter are for fresh yeast and easy-bake yeast, the latter being the type most widely available. Fresh pressed yeast can be bought from high street bakers, sometimes in the bakery sections of supermarkets or in wholefood shops. If you use fresh yeast, the yeast flavour in the bread is often more pronounced; you always need to add twice the amount of fresh yeast in weight.

Baking soda or bicarbonate of soda is used in a few recipes in this chapter in place of yeast. This is the most convenient of all, and you can make bread almost instantly, but these breads have a short life and do not stand reheating for toast except when very fresh.

MORE ABOUT YEAST BAKING

Adding more yeast will not improve bread. It may become active quickly, but the texture of the bread will be poor and cakey and it will taste overwhelmingly of yeast, not grain.

Commercial yeast is killed by salt. More salt can be added to sourdoughs and it has an impact on the slow fermentation, but bought yeast is killed by salt. It is important to stick to the amount of salt specified in the recipe, and no more, otherwise the dough will be 'dead' and won't ferment after mixing. If you add too little salt, however, the bread will taste dull – salt is needed to enhance the flavour of the grain.

Fresh yeast is less active by volume than dried. In this book, yeast in a recipe means 'easy-bake' (quick) dried yeast, unless otherwise specified. Use twice the amount of fresh yeast when the recipe specifies dried, e.g. for 7g/¼oz dried yeast, use 14g/½oz fresh yeast. If you use fresh yeast, always dissolve it in some of the liquid before adding to the mix, letting it stand for 5 minutes to activate and become bubbly.

Enhancing the flavour and texture of bread made with commercial yeast. Regular bakers can improve the bread they make with commercial yeast so that the resulting bread has a chewier texture and more flavour: simply keep 100g/3½oz dough after the first baking, put it in plastic container with a lid in the fridge and use it in the mix when next baking (up to 2 days later or it will be exhausted and lose its activity). Repeat each time you bake.

....

Stages. The process of making bread with 'easy-bake' yeast is done in five phases*:

Stage 1. Mixing the dough

Stage 2. First prove (rise): 1½–2½ hours

Stage 3. Shaping the loaves/rolls

Stage 4. Second prove: 30–60 minutes

Stage 5. Baking the bread or rolls: 20–45 minutes

* If using fresh yeast, there is an extra phase: the fresh yeast must be dissolved first in a little of the liquid.

....

Total time. Minimum 3 hours including kneading and shaping; maximum 4¾ hours. The time it takes depends much on the flour type, the moisture in the dough, the richness (addition of butter and/or eggs) and the ambient temperature. If it is very cool in the kitchen and you have no warm place to leave the dough to prove, the fermentation will be slow. Likewise, the liquid added to the dough must be lukewarm (about 20°C, or up to 29°C) or the dough ferment will be very slow to get going.

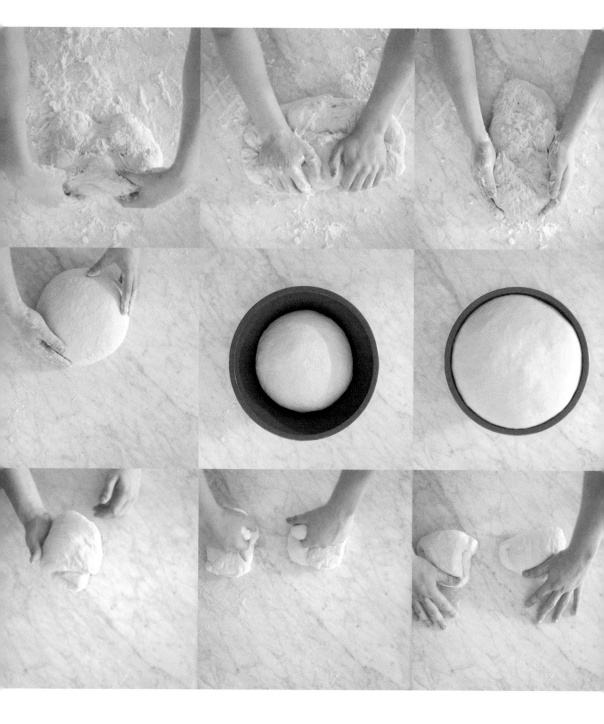

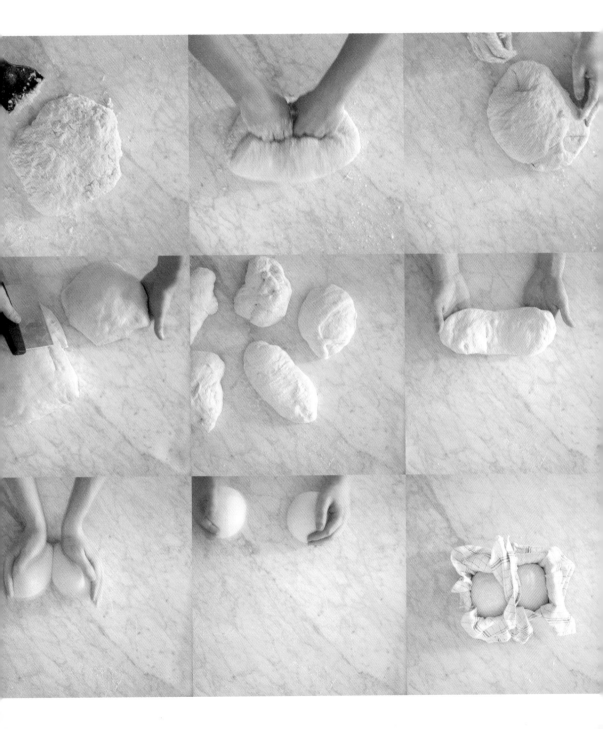

WHITE TIN LOAF

Beginners need a no-fuss, simple loaf recipe to build confidence as a baker. This bread is just that, a take on the typical high-rise, golden, rectangular loaf that makes everyday bread for sandwiches and the toaster.

You can, if time allows, put the dough in the fridge overnight, which slows the fermentation and improves the texture. The following day, take it out and leave for 1 hour to return to room temperature then shape as normal.

Mixing and kneading the dough

Put the flour in a large bowl and rub in the butter or oil (if using). Add the yeast and salt, and mix to distribute it. Pour in the water and mix with your hands or a wooden spoon to a lumpy dough. When well mixed, scoop out the contents of the bowl on to the worktop. Scrape out any extra in the bowl with a dough scraper.

Begin to knead the dough; it will feel quite tight. Stretch it using both hands then fold it, turn it, and stretch again. Do this for a minute or two then leave the dough to rest and soften for 3 minutes. Repeat the kneading action, and resting phase, a few more times until the dough feels smooth and elastic. This takes a minimum of 10 minutes but likely up to 15.

First prove

Form the dough into a ball and put back into the mixing bowl. Cover with cling film and leave in a warm place (about 20–29°C) for 1½–2 hours. The dough will double in size.

Shaping the dough

Remove the dough from the bowl and knead to punch out the air, or 'knock it back'. Cut into two and press each out into an oblong about 20cm wide to fit the tin. Roll up loosely and tuck the ends down towards the join to neaten into an oblong with a smooth surface. Drop into the bread tin and dust lightly with a fine covering of flour.

Second prove

Leave to prove in a warm place, uncovered, for 30–40 minutes until well risen. Be careful not to over-prove – you should feel some resistance when pressing gently with a finger. These loaves should have beautiful domed tops well above the tin (unless you are using larger tins than 20cm, which is fine).

Baking the bread

Preheat the oven to 240°C/475°F/Gas mark 9. Put the loaves in the oven, then, after about 5 minutes turn the heat down to 200°C/400°F/Gas mark 6. Bake until golden brown, about 30 minutes in total, then remove from the oven. Cool on a rack. This bread is lovely warm but allow to cool for about 15 minutes or it will compact when sliced.

Makes 2 loaves, each weighing about 750g/1lb 10oz

Equipment

2 x 450g/1lb loaf tins

Timing

The total proving time is approximately 2¾ hours, plus half an hour for the kneading and shaping and 30–40 minutes baking.

Storage

This bread keeps well for 2 days, and is good for toast for a further 2. For fine breadcrumbs, dry pieces in the oven at a very low temperature, or on a rack in a warm place, then blend in a food processor. Dry breadcrumbs keep for months in a sealed container.

Ingredients

1kg/2lb 2oz strong white flour

30g/1oz softened **butter**, or olive oil*

7g/¼oz **dried yeast** (or 15g/½oz fresh; see page 73)

10g/¼oz salt

650g/1lb 7oz lukewarm **water**

Extra **flour** for dusting

* If you are using stoneground white flour or substituting stoneground wholemeal flour, fat is unnecessary because these flours contain natural oils.

HONEY WHOLEMEAL PLAIT

Hunks of warm brown bread, pulled from a plait then buttered, are made for dipping in soup or serving with herby pork pâtés and vegetable mousses. This is a chance, also, to seek out some properly worthy wholemeal flour, milled in a traditional mill (see Suppliers, page 246), and let its grainy flavour take the central role. Choose a honey with a tangy flavour, like rapeseed or heather, for this bread. You can, if you want, put the dough in the fridge overnight, which slows the fermentation and improves the texture.

Makes 2 x 800g/1lb 12oz loaves

Equipment
Baking sheet lined with baking parchment

Timing
Approximately 4¼ hours, including 2½ hours' proving time.

Storage
Keeps well for 2 days and freezes well.

Ingredients
1kg/2lb 2oz strong wholemeal flour

30g/1oz honey

7g/¼oz dried yeast

650g/1lb 7oz lukewarm water

10g/¼oz salt

Extra flour or rolled or cracked wheat grains for dusting

Mixing and kneading the dough
Put the flour in the bowl and add all the other ingredients. Mix to a dough then tip on to the table, using a scraper to remove all the dough from the bowl. Knead the bread, pushing it with the heel of one hand and stretching it with the other, then folding and repeating. It will feel quite stolid at first, and a little wet, but gradually it will become smooth and soft. Rest it now and again, to let the gluten relax. It will be easier to knead having done this. Total kneading time is about 15 minutes.

First prove
Form the dough into a ball and place back in the bowl. Cover the bowl with cling film and leave to prove in a warm place for 2 hours. The dough should have almost doubled in size.

Shaping the dough
Remove the dough from the bowl and cut into 3 pieces – weigh them to check that they are the same size. Roll each piece into a long sausage the thickness of your thumb. Place the 3 pieces of dough side by side on the baking sheet, but not touching. At one end, tuck the 2 outer strips under the central strip and press to seal. Take one of the outer strips, and bring it across the central strip. Take the opposite strip and bring that across the first strip you moved.

Continue like this, loosely plaiting the dough, until you reach the end of the loaf. Try to finish by tucking the central strip under the bread and pinch to seal.

Second prove

Scatter a light dusting of flour, or rolled or cracked wheat grains (if you have them), over the plaited loaf and leave to prove for 30–45 minutes until well risen. The plait will tighten as it rises.

Baking the bread

Preheat the oven to 220°C/425°F/Gas mark 7. Place the plait in the oven and bake for 35–45 minutes, turning it down to 200°C/400°F/Gas mark 6 after 5 minutes. The loaf is cooked when pale brown and very fragrant. Remove from the oven and cool on a rack. Wrap in a cloth when still warm (but not straight after cooking) to preserve some heat. To eat, simply pull the plait apart at the joins.

BATTERSEA BRIDGE ROLLS

Living so near a bridge on the Thames, we could not resist putting a South London twist on the old name for these glossy, rich picnic rolls so popular in our grandparents' days. Ours are a larger version, and baked in a batch so the sides join on the baking sheet. Split and fill with air-dried ham and peppery salad leaves, or a glossy home-made egg mayonnaise.

Combine the milk with the butter, yeast and beaten eggs. Put the flour, salt and sugar in a large mixing bowl and mix in the milk and yeast mixture. Use your hands/or an electric mixer with a dough hook to knead for at least 5 minutes, or until the dough is smooth and comes away from the side of the bowl.

Cover the bowl with cling film and leave for 1½ hours until the dough rises to double the size.

Knead the dough briefly then use floured hands to divide into 32 roughly equal pieces. Shape into thumb-sized rolls and place on the baking sheets, about 2cm/1 inch apart so the rolls will grow together as the dough inflates.

Leave to prove for 30 minutes. Once swollen and yet still quite firm to touch, brush gently with the glaze.

Preheat the oven to 220°C/425°F/Gas mark 7. Put the glazed rolls into the oven and bake for 15 minutes, turning the oven down to 200°C/400°F/Gas mark 6 after 3 minutes. The rolls are ready when golden brown. Take out of the oven and cool on a rack.

Makes 32 rolls

Equipment

2 x large **baking sheets**, greased or lined with baking parchment

Timing

Approximately 3 hours including 1½ hours' proving time.

Storage

Eat on the day, or freeze for up to 3 weeks.

Ingredients

200ml/7fl oz lukewarm **milk**

60g/2 ¼oz **butter**, melted and cooled to lukewarm

7g/¼oz **dried yeast** (or 15g/½oz fresh; see page 73)

4 **eggs**, beaten

580g/1lb 5oz **strong white flour**

1 teaspoon **salt**

1 tablespoon **caster sugar**

To glaze:

1 **egg**, beaten with 1 tablespoon **water** and 1 pinch **salt**

SAFFRON COILS

Grown-up dinner rolls to eat with dry-cured or smoked meats, made with milk for a softer crumb. Be sure to make a saffron infusion in plenty of time (at least two hours prior to mixing the dough) so that the flavour will have a chance to come through.

Warm the milk then add the saffron. Leave to infuse for at least 2 hours.

Put the flour, salt and butter in a large mixing bowl; rub the butter into the flour and stir in the yeast to distribute it. Add the saffron milk with the water and eggs and mix to a dough. Take the dough out of the bowl, scraping the sides, and knead on the worktop. Stretch and fold it several times, pausing now and again to allow the gluten to relax.

Put the dough back into the bowl and cover it with cling film. Leave in a warm place to prove for 1½ hours.

Remove the dough from the bowl and knock the air out of it. Cut into 12 long strips each weighing the same. Place one on one of the baking sheets and begin to coil from one end. When you reach halfway, stop. Pick up the end of the un-coiled dough and coil it in the opposite direction. You should be left with a double coil. Place the rolls 2cm apart on the baking sheets.

Leave the rolls to prove for 30 minutes until puffed to almost double in size. Brush with egg glaze and scatter a very few grains of coarse sea salt over the surface.

Preheat the oven to 200°C/400°F/Gas mark 6. Bake the saffron coils for 12–15 minutes, until the buns are puffed and golden. Remove from the oven and cool on a rack.

Makes 12

Equipment

2 baking sheets lined with baking parchment

Timing

Approximately 3 hours including 1½–2 hours' proving time.

Storage

Eat on the day; freezes for 2 months.

Ingredients

250ml/9fl oz milk

½ teaspoon saffron threads

675g/1½lb strong white flour

1 teaspoon salt

115g/4oz softened butter

7g/¼oz dried yeast (or 15g/½oz fresh; see page 73)

175ml/6fl oz lukewarm water

2 eggs, beaten

  To glaze and finish:

1 egg, beaten with 1 tablespoon water and 1 pinch salt

A few grains of coarse sea salt

FLAT BREAD

*More instant bread, but made on the hob, not in the oven –
these can be cooked plain, or filled with fresh cheese and herbs
and folded. The base of the dough is yeast-free. When bread
is rolled or stretched very thin it will develop little blisters,
trapping air as it cooks. The flour is very finely milled Italian
flour called '00' (double zero) and is often used for homemade
pasta dough, which needs to be rolled very thinly. Ordinary
plain flour will do, but the dough will be grainier and crisp
when cooked.*

Makes 4 flat breads,
or filled breads

....

Equipment

Large heavy-based frying pan,
or crêpe pan, or a griddle. Asian
homeware shops sometimes
sell 'roti' pans, which are ideal.

....

Timing

Four breads can be made in
an hour, including 30 minutes'
resting time.

....

Storage

Eat within the day. These breads
freeze well wrapped in cling film.

....

Ingredients

150g/5½oz Italian '00' white flour,
sifted

2 tablespoons extra virgin olive oil

½ teaspoon fine salt

75ml/2½fl oz-120ml/4fl oz
ice-cold water

Olive oil for cooking (optional)

Put the flour in a bowl and add the olive oil and salt. Add 75ml/
2½ fl oz of the water and mix until you have a soft, smooth dough,
adding more water if it does not come together. The dough should
be slightly tacky but should not stick to your hands or the bowl. If it
does, add a little more flour. Dust the dough ball lightly with flour,
wrap in cling film and place in the fridge for 30 minutes. If you are
filling the breads, this is the time to prepare the ingredients.

Remove the dough from the fridge and cut into 4 pieces. By now
it should not be tacky at all but soft and pliable. Dust the worktop
with flour then roll one piece into a small disc. By the time it is a
15cm/6-inch disc, it will become tight and resist being rolled further.
Check there is enough flour under the disc of dough for it not to
stick then leave it to rest for 2 minutes. Like bread dough, the gluten
needs to be relaxed for you to roll it further.

Continue to roll out the circle. It is easier to give it a quick 30-degree
turn after rolling back and forth once. Rest for a minute now and
then to relax the dough, and use a little more flour if it is sticking to
the rolling pin. Stop when the disc is about 25cm/10 inches across.

Heat the pan over a medium-high heat. Roll the dough disc on to
the pin, pick it up and unroll onto the pan. The bread will begin to
bubble and blister, turning opaque in places. Lift the bread with a
spatula to see if all the underside is cooked and browned in places. If
some of the blisters are too dark brown, turn the heat down.

Flip the bread over with the spatula and cook on the other side. If you
want the bread to be crisp, brush it with olive oil after flipping it the
first time. Flip it, brush the other side with oil then flip again. Once
cooked, place on a clean tea towel and wrap the bread to keep it soft.

Cheese and herb-filled flat breads

Make the flat breads as per the recipe on the opposite page up to the point where the bread is rolled out to the correct size. Scatter cheese and herbs over one half only, leaving a 1cm/½-inch border free. Brush the edge with water, then lift and fold the other half of the bread to make a semicircle.

Heat the pan, then, using two spatulas or a bread peel, pick up the filled bread and place it on the hot pan. Cook until the underside is opaque and blistered, lightly browned in places. Carefully lift it with the spatulas again and turn it over – this takes a little practice. Brush the surface that has been cooked with olive oil; cook for about 1 minute then flip over again. Brush this second side with olive oil and flip over immediately. Cook for less than a minute, then it is ready to eat. The bread should be crisp in places. It may leak a little but it will still be heavenly, eaten hot. You can cut these breads into wedges to serve with drinks, at room temperature.

For the filling:

225g/8oz feta cheese, crumbled into small pieces

4 tablespoons fresh mint leaves, chopped

4 tablespoons fresh dill leaves, chopped

4 tablespoons fresh coriander leaves, chopped

Olive oil for cooking

Water for sealing

THREE-MINUTE SPELT, APPLE & SEED BREAD

Makes 1 large loaf

Equipment

900g/2lb loaf tin, or 2 x 450g/1lb loaf tins, lined with baking parchment or greased with vegetable oil

Timing

One hour and 3 minutes! Plus a few minutes to gather ingredients, and wash up...

Storage

Keeps well for 2 days. This bread is so good warm that there is unlikely to be much left after one breakfast sitting. It does not benefit from freezing, becoming quite dry with a hard crust.

Ingredients

500g/1lb 2oz spelt flour

10g/¼oz dried yeast

½ teaspoon sea salt

1 small eating apple, grated

55g/2oz sunflower seeds, plus extra for the surface of the loaf

55g/2oz sesame seeds

55g/2oz linseeds

500ml/18fl oz warm water

Improbable but true, some breads need no proving at all. Spelt, a type of wheat grain that dates back over 2,000 years, is unique in the way that it reacts so fast – fermenting quickly on contact with yeast in a wet dough – that it can be baked with no preliminary proving. Once kneaded for three minutes it almost instantly becomes silky smooth and goes into tins for immediate baking. The addition of grated apple and seeds lightens this very healthy bread, which is the kind that is good with cheese, chutney and crisp lettuce.

On one occasion when trying a different brand of spelt flour, the bread emerged from the oven like a brick. The only conclusion to reach was that the flour was not pure spelt but ordinary wholemeal wheat. See the Suppliers section (page 246) for a source of pure spelt flour.

Preheat the oven to 200°C/400°F/Gas mark 6. Combine all the ingredients in a bowl. Mix well – the dough will be very wet – then scoop it into the tin. Scatter over a few sunflower seeds and put in the oven right away. Bake for 1 hour, until the loaf has risen. It is done when it comes out of the tin with ease and feels lighter for its size. Cook for another 5 minutes, out of the tin, then remove from the oven and allow to cool.

WHEATEN SODA BREAD

Soda bread is instant baking gratification. A quick mix, into the oven and little more than 30 minutes later you have bread to melt hearts. The scent of warm grain, a crumb softened by buttermilk, the sweetness of malt contrasting with a slight lemony acidity – this is bread that delivers much for very little effort. But its appeal is fleeting. This is bread to make on the day and eat as it cools, which is not difficult given that it is perfectly practical to make it for supper after a day at work. Day-old soda bread neither tastes good or toasts well.

The most inexperienced baker can make good soda bread. If there is a limit to its success, however, it is simply that it needs good flour. White flour soda bread needs good, unbleached stoneground flour, but the favourite, surely, is wheaten soda bread with properly grainy flour. This is a combination of fine-milled wholemeal with the addition of crushed whole wheat. You can also add other grains, such as oats, rye and cornmeal, but there must be a gluten element (from a conventional wheat flour) to lighten the bread.

Preheat the oven to 220°C/425°F/Gas mark 7. Put all the ingredients in a bowl and swiftly mix together. Turn the dough out on to the worktop and lightly knead for a minute, using dough scrapers if it is very sticky (wet is good in this case). The dough will be activated by the soda very quickly and unless it is mixed and baked as soon as possible it can be heavy.

Transfer the dough to the tin or mould. Smooth the surface with wet fingers and scatter plenty of rolled oats on top. Bake for 25–35 minutes until risen and golden.

Makes 1 loaf, about 800g/1lb 12oz

Equipment
1kg/2lb **loaf tin** or wooden mould (see Suppliers, page 246), lined with baking parchment

Timing
30–40 minutes

Storage
This bread doesn't keep. It needs to be eaten on the day it's made.

Ingredients
400g/14oz **wheaten flour**＊

50g/1¾oz **rolled oats**, plus extra for the surface of the loaf

1 tablespoon **malt** or molasses

2 teaspoons **bicarbonate of soda**

1½ teaspoons **salt**

400ml **buttermilk** or whole milk soured with 1 tablespoon lemon juice

＊ See Suppliers, page 246, for sources of wheaten flour, or mix 100g/3½oz kibbled wheat (rye or ordinary wheat) into 300g/10½oz best stoneground wholemeal flour.

POLENTA BREAD WITH SAGE & BACON

This is a simple-to-make soda bread, based on the cornbreads made in the United States of America that are often placed on the tables still in the pan they were cooked in. It is lovely bread to eat fresh, with a salad of ripe tomatoes, for example, but we like it best sliced, fried or grilled, and served with roast poultry in place of bread sauce, or with roast pork. It has an extraordinary capacity to soak up gravy. For a gritty texture, use natural polenta meal, not instant.

Preheat the oven to 200°C/400°F/Gas mark 6. Fry the sage and bacon in 1 tablespoon of the butter until light brown, then add to the cornmeal. Rub the rest of the butter into the cornmeal then add the flour, sugar, baking powder, salt and bicarbonate of soda.

The buttermilk and egg should be added only when you are ready to bake – this is so that all the airy bubbles created by the baking powder and soda do not collapse. Stir into the mixture briefly, enough that all the ingredients are well mixed but not overworked. Quickly transfer into the loaf tin or pan, then bake for 20–25 minutes until well risen and golden brown. Test with a skewer – if it comes out clean the cornbread is ready.

Once cool, store wrapped in aluminium foil until needed. Cut into 1cm/½-inch slices, then fry in either duck fat, dripping or olive oil.

Makes 1 loaf, serving 8–10 as part of a meal

Equipment

1kg/2lb baking tin – either a loaf tin or a round ovenproof pan – lined with baking parchment and buttered well

Timing

50 minutes

Storage

Best eaten on the day but if wrapped in foil, this loaf can be sliced and grilled or fried, 3 days after making.

Ingredients

1 tablespoon chopped sage leaves

2 rashers smoked streaky bacon, cut into small squares

125g/4½oz softened butter

375g/13oz natural polenta (corn/maize) meal

250g/9oz plain flour

1 teaspoon sugar

1½ teaspoons baking powder

1 teaspoon salt

½ teaspoon bicarbonate of soda

250ml/9fl oz buttermilk

3 large eggs, beaten

FOLDED BREADS

A loaf made from weak flour that will never rise high, into which we stuff anything that seems right on the day or comes into season. The texture is bubbly – we allow this bread deliberately to over-prove – and the bread is soft to bite.

Put half the flour in a bowl with all the water and 3g/⅛oz of the yeast. Mix well to make a wet batter. Cover with cling film and place in the fridge overnight. This method helps develop the flavour and texture of the bread.

Remove the bowl from the fridge the next day and allow the mixture to come to room temperature. Work in the remaining flour, yeast and salt then put it (preferably) in a stand mixer. Beat, adding the olive oil slowly, then continuously, for about 8 minutes until the dough is coming away from the side of the mixing bowl and looks stringy and tacky. If the dough is too dry or wet, add a little water or flour to correct.

Place in a bowl and leave to prove for 2 hours at room temperature. Once well risen, scrape the dough gently out of the bowl onto a well-floured surface. Cut it in half with a knife – the object is not to disturb the bubbles in the bread too much. There is no need to shape it; it will spread naturally into a flat shape.

Preheat the oven (with the pizza stone, if using) to 200°C/400°F/ Gas mark 6. Scatter the filling (see below) over one half of each piece of dough. Fold the other side over it, dust the surface with flour and leave to prove for 35–45 minutes (either on a very well-floured worktop, if you are baking on stone, or on the baking sheet), until well risen and large bubbles are visible. Put the bread in the oven before the bubbles pop, or it may not rise much in the oven.

Ideas for fillings

Add approximately 300g filling to each loaf, combining ingredients as you like:

- Walnuts and raisins, plus a teaspoon of scattered cinnamon and brown sugar

- Fresh goat's cheese, basil leaves and roasted artichokes

- Roasted cherry tomatoes, with olive oil and oregano

- Sweet cooked onion and garlic

- Woody herbs – rosemary, thyme and sage – with chopped pork crackling

- Soaked dried figs, with dates, sultanas, pistachio and thyme honey.

Makes 2 x 800g/1lb 12oz (approximate weight) loaves

. . . .

Equipment

Pizza stone or baking stone with baker's peel, or a baking sheet lined with baking parchment

. . . .

Timing

3½ hours

. . . .

Ingredients

750g/1lb 10oz plain white or Italian '00' white flour

500ml/18fl oz water

7g/¼oz dried yeast or 15g/½oz fresh (see page 73)

10g/¼oz salt

115g/4oz olive oil

Rich bread

We are in the favourite territory of all bread lovers, the land of rich, soft crumb, of tall loaves and plump buns enriched with butter and eggs. These breads are a joy to make and fill the home with the intoxicating scent of baked cinnamon and lemon overlaid with the aroma of enveloping, warm dough. Some are easy to make, others must be made with uncompromising rule book in hand, but all invite creativity: once you have the master recipes for the dough, shape it any way you want it; twist and fold, roll and fill – or pack into an unusual mould. Welcome to the dominion of buns, babas and brioche – it is a very delicious one.

On the sober side, the challenge when making dough heavy with butter and eggs is to make the result light. If that is a paradox, stay with us because there are ways to make sure this happens. You have to be a little more patient with rich dough. Even though made with fast-acting commercial yeast, this dough will not blossom into expanded dough just like that. Because fresh ingredients are added such as eggs and butter, this dough benefits from being proved at a low temperature, very slowly, in the fridge. Which is logical – this dough

must be kept stable, meaning that too much warmth at proving time could turn the butter sour. A wrongly made brioche can taste piteously rancid – all that work, gone to waste.

Yet, in a bid to encourage those put off by the timing element, the slowness of the process is not about the baker having to do more work, merely extra idle time for the dough to go through a safe ferment. The actual work involved in manufacture is minimal, though a stand mixer is highly recommended for those without strong arms. I would go so far as to say that recipes in this chapter containing a high degree of butter and eggs, like brioche, cannot be made without machinery because the motorised whipping motions of such machines give the finished dough incredible elasticity. There are, though, for those without machines or even elbow grease, other simple buns like babas to try, which are perfectly suited to being hand made.

This kind of baking can be extravagant. Our flower pot brioche has been a Pocket Bakery bestseller; whenever we put them out they are snapped up instantly. But perhaps I should admit that we often make very little selling them. Brioche needs one special ingredient in particular: the finest butter, which is never cheap.

You should be able to taste the butter in the finished bun, or you will be eating something that is rich but for no especial gain in terms of savour. It is very noticeable that a factory-made brioche too often tastes of 'butter flavour' and contains yellow colouring. If you do decide to make rich buns commercially, it is going to be necessary to source butter that is suitable and affordable (see Suppliers, page 246).

If all this sounds a touch stern, just remember that once you are familiar with the process and can set about making a batch of rich breads with your eyes closed, you will make certain, small people very happy. When I was a child and we holidayed with my grandmother who lived in France, she only allowed us one brioche a week at Sunday breakfast. We called them 'bunnies' – they were dusted with delicious, crunchy 'nibbed' sugar. Waking up on a Sunday morning was always all the nicer.

MORE ABOUT BUNS, BABAS & BRIOCHE

The mantra is 'cool'. Phrases like 'softened' (butter) and 'lukewarm' (milk) or warmed bowls are out of date and make the process more likely to fail. Follow recipes for rich breads keeping all ingredients cool: the flour (obviously), the butter, eggs and milk. There is no need to bring things to room temperature. The easy way to obtain 'cool but soft' butter is to take it straight from the fridge, place it between two sheets of greaseproof paper and bash it with a rolling pin to soften it ready for use. After that, cut it with a knife into small pieces.

Use better butter. Experience has taught us that the better the butter the greater the result. Unsalted butter is the type asked for in recipes, which can be tasteless unless you choose a type that has a ripe flavour. French butter is reliable, remaining stable even when beaten in an electric mixer, because it is lactic, i.e. thickened with the use of a culture that delivers that rounded ripe taste. There are suitable British butters (see Suppliers, page 246). Lactic butter is also more stable than typical British 'sweetcream' butter, which can be-come greasy when beaten at high speed. Like me you might become butter-obsessive and keep an eye out for new types to try.

Golden eggs. An egg with a deep yellow-coloured yolk will not have much impact on texture or taste but it does make a gorgeous, sunshiny crumb in a bun or brioche. For eggs with darker yolks, see Suppliers (page 246), or look out for farmers' market/farm-gate sales of eggs from Maran or Welsummer hens.

The slowest brioche. You can make brioche with a sourdough, but obviously the yeasts in sourdough are much less active and the ferment for a rich dough, which again must be refrigerated, has to be in the fridge for at least 18 hours. Likewise, the second prove, after shaping, may be hours long, in a cool place, of course. For one quantity of the master brioche recipe on page 101, substitute 30g/1oz sourdough starter for the commercial yeast. You may need to reduce the liquid quantity in the recipe by about 15ml because adding the sourdough will increase the moisture content. With buns, the same applies but the dough will not need to be proved in the fridge.

Patient proving. A watched brioche or bun never proves. Once the overnight prove is done, and the brioche or buns are shaped and proving the second time at room temperature – give them all the time they need. The dough will rise, and just when you think it has grown as much as it can, it manages another centimetre or two. Keep an eye on it, making sure the dough is not falling or becoming exhausted. Do not put in a warm (above 25°C) place, or it may rise quickly and collapse.

TIMING

STORAGE

Most rich bun doughs are best made the day before and baked the next morning. The richer the dough, the more a night's slow proving in the fridge benefits the result. For brioche, make the dough late in the afternoon or early evening for baking the next morning, for breakfast.

Brioche is best eaten fresh on the day of baking, but makes lovely toast for two further days. It also freezes well if frozen when fresh.

The process of making brioche dough follows five stages:

Stage 1. Mix and knead the dough

Stage 2. First prove – in the refrigerator

Stage 3. Shape the buns and loaves

Stage 4. Second prove

Stage 5. Bake the buns and loaves

FLOWER POT BRIOCHE

Not everyone has a fluted brioche mould, but most can beg or borrow a couple of terracotta pots when making a first attempt at this soft-hearted bread that is fragrant with butter – the flute shape of a flower pot is just the job. Tips for success: this is not a recipe to attempt without a stand mixer or very big biceps. Also, use French or other lactic butter because it stays sweetly stable when worked. We find, sad to say, most British butter tends to become greasy and rancid in brioche. This recipe makes a sturdy brioche that will rise high.

Stage 1. Mixing and kneading the dough

Put the flour in the mixing bowl, add the salt and mix briefly (use the beater attachment). Add the yeast to the warm milk with the sugar and mix until the yeast has dissolved. Add to the mixing bowl with the beaten eggs.

Mix at a low speed for 3 minutes. The dough will be very firm, tacky and pale yellow in colour.

Keeping the mixer on slow, add the butter pieces, one by one, a few seconds apart so they are incorporated into the dough. You may find this takes a while, and you need to stop the mixer from time to time and scrape down the sides with a spatula and break up any large clods of butter.

The dough will become increasingly elastic, glossy and begin to leave the sides of the bowl clean. Turn off the mixer, scrape down the sides of the bowl again and cover with cling film.

Stage 2. First prove – in the refrigerator

Leave in the fridge overnight. During this slow prove, the mixture will double in size.

Stage 3. Shaping the buns and loaves

Remove from the fridge and leave at room temperature until it feels softer to the touch – about 1–1½hours. The dough is now ready to be shaped. It will be soft and sticky so use floured hands to divide into 6 pieces. Divide each of these into 3 pieces and drop each lot of 3 into one flowerpot – this ensures there is a little air trapped in the dough in each pot, allowing it to expand better and so there is no doughy centre to the brioche once cooked.

Stage 4. Second prove

Once you have filled the pots, brush the surface of each one with egg wash and leave to prove for 45 minutes.

Stage 5. Baking the buns and loaves

Just before baking, brush with egg wash once more. Bake at 200°C/ 400°F/Gas mark 6 for approximately 20–25 minutes, or until deep gold in colour.

Larger flower pot brioche

After removing the dough from the fridge after the overnight prove and allowing it to soften at room temperature, divide the brioche dough in two and proceed as for the smaller flower pots. Larger brioche will need a longer second prove before baking and could take up to 40 minutes to cook at 180°C/350°F/Gas mark 4. Test to see if they are done by inserting a skewer and drawing it out, as you would a cake. If the skewer comes out clean, the brioche is cooked.

Makes 6 small flower pot brioches, each enough for one person

Equipment

Stand mixer fitted with a dough hook (an electric hand mixer is not powerful enough)

6 small flower pots (10cm/4 inches wide)

6 x 15x23cm/6x9-inch pieces of baking parchment

Timing

3 hours (excluding overnight prove)

Ingredients

500g plain white flour

1 teaspoon fine salt

20g/scant 1oz fresh yeast or 10g/ scant ¼oz dried

60ml whole milk, lukewarm

1 tablespoon sugar

6 eggs, beaten

350g butter from the fridge, cut into 2cm/¾inch dice

For the egg wash:

1 egg, beaten with 1 tablespoon sugar and 1 pinch salt

CLASSIC BRIOCHE LOAF

This is the brioche to eat with savoury foods: with potted chicken liver mousse, or dry-cured ham. Make it in a loaf tin, as you would bread for sandwiches. It has a close texture inside, but the surface is often appealingly rough, like a golden crown.

Take the dough from the fridge and allow it to come to room temperature (about 1–1½ hours). Form the dough into an oblong (or 2 if you are making 2 smaller loaves), trying not to lose all the air in the dough.

Place the dough in the tin (or tins). Brush with egg wash. They will grow as they prove.

Leave the dough to prove for about 1 hour, until well risen. Then brush with egg wash again and bake at 180°C/350°F/Gas mark 4 until burnished and crisp. Remove from the oven; allow to cool in the tin before removing.

Makes one large loaf (1kg/2lb) or 2 small (500g/1lb) loaves

Equipment

1kg/2lb loaf tin, or 2 x 500g/1lb tins, lightly greased

Ingredients

1 quantity Brioche dough (page 101) prepared to the end of stage 2 (mixed and proved overnight in the fridge)

For the egg wash:

1 egg, beaten with 1 tablespoon sugar and 1 pinch salt

FRESH FRUIT BRIOCHE 'SANDWICH' WITH BERRIES & CREAM

This is a brioche layer cake; we daresay much better than any other cream cake filled with strawberries.

Take the dough from the fridge and allow it to come to room temperature (about 1–1½ hours). Shape it into one large ball on a floured surface – gently so as not to lose the air. Roll it into a circle 25cm/10-inch across and place on the baking sheet, inside the tart ring. Alternatively put it in a cake tin. Brush with egg wash and leave to prove for 1–1½ hours until risen well but not beginning to fall.

Preheat the oven to 180°C/350°F/Gas mark 4. Scatter the nibbed sugar over the surface. Bake for 30 minutes or until golden and crisp.

Remove from the oven and slide the baked brioche disc on to a rack. Allow to cool. Once it is completely cool, cut the cake horizontally in two and fill with strawberries and whipped cream.

Serves 6–8

Equipment

25cm/10-inch **tart ring** and a **baking sheet**, or a similar size **cake tin**

Ingredients

¾ quantity **Brioche dough** (page 101) prepared to the end of stage 2 (mixed and proved overnight in the fridge); use remainder to make some Bunnies (page 107)

For the egg wash:

1 **egg**, beaten with 1 tablespoon **sugar** and 1 pinch **salt**

60g/2 ¼oz **nibbed sugar** (Suppliers, page 246)

For the filling:

300ml/½ pint **whipped cream**

500g/1lb 2oz **strawberries**, hulled and sliced in half

BUNNIES

The small brioche breakfast buns of my childhood; slightly wonky and covered with sugar.

Take the dough from the fridge and allow it to come to room temperature (about 1–1½ hours). Cut it into 24 pieces – do not shape the pieces into rounds, they are nicer with a rough surface. Place a piece in each mould of the muffin tray. Scatter the nibbed sugar over the surface and leave to prove for 30–45 minutes.

Preheat the oven to 180°C/350°F/Gas mark 4. When the bunnies have risen to the fullest, bake for 15–25 minutes until golden and crisp. Cool on a rack – you can serve them as they are, with jam on the table, or split them and fill with fresh blueberries and cream, or raspberry jam and clotted cream.

Makes about 24 x 50g buns

Equipment

2 x 12-hole **muffin trays**, lightly greased with butter

Ingredients

1 quantity **Brioche dough** (page 101) prepared to the end of stage 2 (mixed and proved overnight in the fridge)

For the egg wash and sugar:

1 **egg**, beaten with 1 tablespoon **sugar** and 1 pinch **salt**

85g/3oz **nibbed sugar** (Suppliers, page 246)

CHOCOLATE TWINS

Inspired by gemelli pasta twists, these brioche buns are studded with hidden chocolate twists.

Take the dough from the fridge and allow it to come to room temperature (about 1–1½ hours). Cut into 16 more or less equal strips. Lay them on a lightly floured board and stick good quality chocolate nibs along the length of them, studding them into the dough at 3cm intervals.

Brush with egg wash then – this can be slightly messy – bring one end up to meet the other and twist the two ends together like a rope.

Lay the twins on the baking sheet and brush with more egg wash. Leave to prove for 35–45 minutes.

Preheat the oven to 180°C/350°F/Gas mark 4. When the twists have risen to their fullest, bake for 20 minutes or until golden and crisp. Cool on a rack – but it is nice to eat these warm while the chocolate is still soft.

Makes 16

Equipment

1 large **baking sheet**, lightly greased with butter

Ingredients

1 quantity **Brioche dough** (page 101) prepared to the end of stage 2 (mixed and proved overnight in the fridge)

300g dark or milk **chocolate nibs**

For the egg wash:

1 **egg**, beaten with 1 tablespoon **sugar** and 1 pinch **salt**

SWEET OLIVE OIL BREADS WITH WINE GRAPES & ANISE

These not-too-sweet breads are heavily enriched with olive oil, and good eaten as part of a picnic with dry-cured ham, salami and soft cheeses. Red wine grapes may be too much to ask for but the proliferation of vineyards in the south of England might make them easier pickings for locals. Otherwise, look for Muscat grapes in supermarkets in autumn, or ripe black grapes. The point of wine grapes is the thinness of their skins, which rupture quickly in the oven, dramatically leaking black juice into these breads. A winemaker might add 'must', the leftovers from the wine-making, to this bread – in sparing quantities.

Makes 8

Equipment
2 baking sheets, lightly greased

Ingredients

For the sponge ferment:

3g/½ teaspoon fresh yeast or 2g dried

150g/5½oz water

150g/5oz strong white flour

For the dough:

1 quantity of sponge ferment

3g/¼oz dried yeast

180g/6 ½oz Italian '00' white flour

60ml/4 tablespoons extra virgin olive oil

5g/1 teaspoon sea salt

To finish:

450g/1lb very ripe black grapes

5g/1 teaspoon aniseed

Leaves from a sprig of rosemary

A small amount of extra virgin olive oil

Caster sugar for dusting

Put all the sponge ferment ingredients into a bowl, mix well, and leave to ferment for 1 hour at room temperature.

Put the dough ingredients, including the sponge ferment, into the bowl of the electric stand mixer and beat for about 10 minutes. Cover the bowl with cling film and place in the fridge overnight.

The following day, take the dough from the fridge – it will be bubbly and firm. Allow to come to room temperature (about 30 minutes) then scrape it out of the bowl on to a floured worktop and cut it into 8, without losing too many bubbles. Press each piece out into a thin 12cm/5-inch circle – again, just use your fingertips; it is good to retain some of the air in the dough. Use extra flour if it is sticky, and then place each on the baking sheets, side by side.

Scatter a few grapes, a tiny pinch of aniseed and some rosemary leaves on to each disc of dough. Shake over a little olive oil. Leave to prove for 30–40 minutes.

Preheat the oven to 240°C/475°F/Gas mark 9. Put the breads in the oven, immediately turn it down to 220°C/425°F/Gas mark 7 and bake for 10–15 minutes or until the dough is pale brown and the grapes blistering.

Remove from the oven. Leave to cool on a rack for a few minutes then scatter over the caster sugar.

CARAMELISED RADICCHIO & WINTER RHUBARB ROUND

Radicchio is a bitter-flavoured leaf but if very slowly cooked it becomes as sweet as fruit and can be added to fruity breads –it is sometimes added to panettone in Italy. In this instance it is kneaded into an enriched dough with winter rhubarb to make a loaf with an interesting pinkish-buff-coloured crumb. This has a wet dough that collapses into a flattish, round bread; a wonderful bread to eat with hard cheeses, slices of apple and chutney.

Put all the sponge ferment ingredients into a bowl, mix well and leave to ferment for 1 hour at room temperature.

The rhubarb and radicchio can be prepared ready to use in the next stage – allowing cooling time. Preheat the oven to 200°C/400°F/Gas mark 6. Put the rhubarb on the lined baking sheet and place the pieces of rhubarb on it, 1cm/½ inch apart. Bake for about 30 minutes, until they have roasted but are not browning. Some juice will leach out and evaporate.

Put the radicchio in a frying pan with the butter and 1 tablespoon of water, and cook over a very low heat for about 15 minutes, until the radicchio is dark brown and tastes sweet. It must not burn, but it will lose its red colour.

Put the dough ingredients, including the sponge ferment, into the bowl of an electric stand mixer and beat for about 10 minutes. Remove the dough from the bowl to a floured worktop using dough scrapers. Scatter the rhubarb and radicchio over two-thirds of the surface. Fold into 3, like a letter, using floured dough scrapers to lift the dough. Pat the dough gently then fold again. Repeat one more time. Put the dough back into the bowl, cover with cling film and place in the fridge overnight.

The following day, take the dough from the fridge. It will be bubbly and firm. Scrape it out of the bowl on to the worktop then lift one edge with a scraper, bringing it into the centre. Repeat, working around the piece of dough, by which time you will have a neat round.

Pick up the dough, turn it over so the smooth side is uppermost, and place it on the greased baking sheet. Dust it with a light covering of flour, if it is not already quite floury. Leave to prove for 1 hour, until well risen.

Preheat the oven to 200°C/400°F/Gas mark 6. Before baking, make a series 4 of shallow slashes on the surface of the round with a blade, like a windmill. Bake for 20–30 minutes or until pale brown and airy. Cool on the baking sheet, then eat sliced.

Makes 2 x 500g/1lb 2oz loaves

Equipment

2 x baking sheets, 1 lined with baking parchment (for the rhubarb), 1 lightly greased

Ingredients

For the sponge ferment:

3g/½ teaspoon fresh yeast or 2g dried

150g/5½oz water

150g/5oz strong white flour

For the filling:

300g/9oz pink winter (forced) rhubarb, cut into 4cm/1½-inch pieces

300g/9oz radicchio leaves, shredded

A nut of butter

For the dough:

1 quantity of sponge ferment (above)

3g/¼oz yeast

180g/6½oz Italian '00' white flour, plus extra for dusting

60ml/4 tablespoons extra virgin or rapeseed oil

5g sea salt

RICH BUNS

From hot cross buns to new inventions filled with figs and honey, these are the buns made with strong bread flour, enriched with egg and butter, that embody a treat. They are less rich than brioche, contain less fat, and the dough is much easier to handle for beginners. I feel they are typically a British sort of bun, the sort I have loved since childhood when every high street had an independent bakery where iced and fruit buns would be displayed delectably on sloping glass shelving in the shop's window. You'd just pray your mother would stop to buy some, every time you passed ...

Rich buns are made with strong white flour, because they need – usually – to rise unsupported and a plain flour makes a very flat, sad bun. Use stoneground white or brown flour where possible. The natural oils in stoneground flour are great for flavour and texture, helping you avoid buns with a cakey crumb.

The dough itself is ready to bake in five relatively quick and easy stages, and the lower richness factor means it does not need to be refrigerated overnight but can be mixed, kneaded, proven, shaped and baked in under three hours.

Stage 1. Mixing and kneading the dough

Stage 2. Proving the dough

Stage 3. Shaping the buns

Stage 4. Proving the buns

Stage 5. Baking the buns

FIG & HONEY COILS

Coils of dough, stuffed with fruit, jammed together snug in a tin, that rise high and appetisingly and are finished with a sprinkling of sugar. Inside each roll, there are velvety ribbons of dough. These rolls follow the principle of Chelsea buns, and you can adapt the recipe to make these or include your favourite preserved fruits, nuts or nibs of toffee or chocolate.

Sift 250g/9oz of the flour into a bowl then add the yeast and caster sugar and whisk to distribute. Add the milk, vanilla and beaten egg then mix to a wet dough. Cover with a cloth and leave in a draught-free spot to rise for about 1 hour until doubled in size.

Add the rest of the flour with the salt and knead on the worktop with your hands until you have a smooth dough. Put back in the bowl and rest the dough for 5 minutes. Repeat this 'knead and rest' technique twice, then scatter the diced butter over the dough, fold the dough and knead to work the butter into it. Rest the dough again – it will be very 'active' and elastic – then fold it and place in the bowl for one further hour. Again it will double in size.

To make the buns, place the dough on a lightly floured work surface and roll to a rectangle measuring 45x30cm/18x12 inches. Brush melted butter over the dough leaving 2cm along one short edge of the dough clear, and drizzle the honey over the surface.

Mix together the sliced softened figs, spice and most of the citrus zest. Scatter evenly over the surface of the dough. Use a little water to wet the border that has not been buttered (to seal the buns) and then roll up the dough from the opposite side to make a 'Swiss roll' measuring 30cm/12 inches.

Cut the roll into 12 pieces and place 3 rows of 4 on the baking tray – so they fit snugly. Leave to prove for a final time until well risen: 30–45 minutes.

Preheat the oven to 180°C/350°F/Gas mark 4. Bake until golden and puffed. Remove and cool in the tin.

Meanwhile, make the glaze. Put the orange juice and honey in a pan and boil until reduced to 2 tablespoons. Brush this over the cooled buns then scatter over the Demerara sugar.

Makes 12

Equipment

1 roasting dish 5cm/2 inches deep and measuring approximately 25x20cm/8x10 inches, the base lined with a sheet of baking parchment then greased with butter

Storage

Eat on the day they are made, or freeze when fresh.

Ingredients

500g/1lb 2oz **strong white flour**

14g/½oz **dried yeast**

55g/2¼oz **caster sugar**

265ml/9½fl oz lukewarm **milk**

½ teaspoon **vanilla extract**

1 **egg**, lightly beaten

7g/¼oz **salt**

55g/2¼oz **butter**, cut into small dice, plus extra 30g/1oz, melted, for brushing

2 tablespoons **clear honey**

250g/9oz **dried figs**, softened in water then sliced

1 teaspoon ground **mixed spice**

Zest of 1 **lemon** and 1 **orange**

For the glaze and finish:

Juice of 1 **orange**

3 tablespoons **honey**

1 heaped tablespoon **Demerara sugar**

ICED FRUIT BUNS

Jack paid me a double-edged compliment when I first made these buns, saying they were like a 'sort of healthy Krispy Kreme'. He was, I realise now, only alluding to their softness under a layer of thin icing.

Makes 12 buns

Equipment
1 baking sheet lined with baking parchment

Storage
Best eaten on the day. If frozen when fresh, they keep very well.

Ingredients
500g/1lb 2oz **strong white flour**, plus extra for dusting

5g/⅛oz fine **salt**

90g/3¼oz softened **butter**

2 level teaspoons ground **cinnamon**

Zest of half an **orange**

Zest of half a **lemon**

150g/5½oz **raisins**

7g/¼oz **dried yeast** or 15g/½oz fresh

500ml/18fl oz **whole milk**, heated until lukewarm

60g/2oz **caster sugar**

3 **egg yolks**

For the icing:

150g **icing sugar**

Approximately 4–5 teaspoons **water**, to make icing the thickness of double cream

Put the flour and salt in a large mixing bowl and quickly rub in the butter. Add the cinnamon, citrus zest and raisins and set to one side.

Stir the yeast into the warm milk until dissolved, then beat in the sugar and egg yolks. Add the yeast mixture to the flour mixture and mix well to form a dough. Dust your hands and the counter with extra flour, scrape the dough out of the bowl on to the counter and knead it, stretching and pulling until it is soft and elastic. This will take about 10 minutes; rest the dough periodically during kneading – this makes it more relaxed and elastic.

Put the dough back in the bowl, cover with cling film and leave at room temperature for 1½–2 hours or until doubled in size.

Remove from the bowl, knocking the air out of the dough, then cut into 12 equal-sized pieces. Using your hand in a claw shape, roll each piece of dough in a circular motion until you have a neat round ball. Arrange the dough balls in a 'batch' on the baking sheet, about 3cm/1 inch apart (they will expand and adhere to each other when proving/baking).

Leave the buns to prove, uncovered, in a warm place for about 40 minutes. Preheat the oven to 200°C/400°F/Gas mark 6. When the buns are risen to double the size and have come together in a batch, bake them for about 15–20 minutes until pale brown.

Cool for 5 minutes on the baking sheet then slide the batch on to a rack or board. To make the icing, mix together the icing sugar and the water in a small bowl. When the buns are cool, paint generously with the icing.

HOT CROSS GOLDEN BUNS

'Golden' due to the lovely yellow sultanas, a type of dried fruit that is becoming easier to find and one of my favourite baking ingredients. They have a lovely lemony flavour, quite different from the robustness of raisins.

Everything is about making hot cross buns for Easter, but doing the crosses themselves – a fuss of handling sweet shortcrust pastry – is a cross to bear. Don't be tempted to use anything else, however: a water paste sweetened with sugar is unpleasant to eat, and just as much of a fiddle. Some books say to use marzipan but I find it melts and burns. The only thing is sweet pastry, draped loosely across the buns so as not to shrink to nothing. Feel free to buy ready-made, or make it to the recipe on page 138.

You need 'strong' wheat flour in order to 'strengthen' the dough, which contains creamy milk (don't use semi-skimmed) plus butter and eggs. I do not, after pleas from my children, add chopped mixed peel to hot cross or other fruit buns, using grated citrus zest instead, but if you love it, add 2 tablespoons and remove the citrus zest in the recipe.

Put the flour and salt in a large mixing bowl and quickly rub in the butter. Add the spices, citrus zest and golden sultanas, and set to one side. Stir the yeast into the lukewarm milk until dissolved then add the sugar and egg. Add the milk mixture to the bowl containing the dry ingredients, mix well to form a dough and use a scraper to tip the contents on to the worktop.

Knead well, stretching and pulling the dough until it is soft and elastic. After 2–3 minutes' kneading, break for 2 minutes to allow the dough to relax and soften. Then knead again. The whole process will take about 10 minutes.

Put the dough back in the bowl, cover with cling film and leave at room temperature for 1½–2 hours or until doubled in size. Remove from the bowl, knocking the air out of the dough, then cut into 12 equal-sized pieces. Use the flat of your hand to roll into neat orbs, then place about 4cm apart on the baking sheet.

Leave the buns to prove, uncovered, in a warm place until doubled in size again – for about 40 minutes to 1 hour. Roll out the sweet pastry and cut into strips 15cm/5 inches long and ½cm/¼-inch wide. Stick crosses to the surface of the bun with a little milk.

Preheat the oven to 200°C/400°F/Gas mark 6 and bake for about 10 minutes until golden brown. Cool on a rack. When cool, brush with the sticky glaze and leave it to set. The buns are ready to eat immediately.

Makes 12 large buns

Equipment

1 **baking sheet**, greased or lined with baking parchment

Storage

All are best eaten on the day but toast well. If frozen when fresh, they keep very well.

Ingredients

500g/1lb 2oz **strong white flour**

5g/¼oz **fine salt**

90g/3¼oz softened **butter**

1 teaspoon **ground cinnamon**

1 teaspoon **mixed spice**

½ teaspoon **ground mace**

Zest of half an **orange**

Zest of half a **lemon**

100g/3½oz **golden sultanas**

30g/1oz **fresh yeast** or 15g dried

300ml/½ pint **whole milk**, heated until lukewarm

60g/2¼oz **caster sugar**

1 **egg**, beaten

200g/7oz **sweet pastry** (page 138)

For the sticky glaze:

5 tablespoons **milk** mixed with 60g **caster sugar** until dissolved

ORANGE STICKY BUNS

Responsible mothers look away now. These are long buns with an outrageous amount of icing to which we can't resist adding some decoration of old-fashioned feather patterns.

Makes 10 buns

. . . .

Equipment

1 baking sheet, lightly greased or lined with baking parchment

Piping bag with fine plain nozzle or a simple freezer bag to improvise

. . . .

Storage

Best eaten on the day. If frozen when fresh, they keep well.

. . . .

Ingredients

515g/1lb 2½oz strong white flour

5g/⅛oz fine salt

90g/3¼oz softened butter

2 teaspoons orange flower water

15g/½oz fresh yeast or 7g/¼oz dried

300ml/½ pint whole milk, heated until lukewarm

60g/2oz caster sugar

3 egg yolks

For the icing:

250g icing sugar

2 tablespoons sieved orange juice

1 teaspoon orange colouring paste

Put the flour and salt in a bowl and rub in the butter. Put the flower water, yeast, milk, caster sugar and egg yolks into a bowl and whisk to dissolve the yeast.

Add the milk mixture to the bowl with the dry ingredients. Mix to a dough then use a dough scraper to turn the mixture out on to the worktop.

Knead well, stretching and pulling the dough until it is soft and elastic. After 2–3 minutes' kneading, break for 2 minutes to allow the dough to relax and soften. Then knead again. The whole process will take about 10 minutes.

Put the dough back in the bowl, cover with cling film and leave to prove for 1½ to 2 hours until well risen. Take the dough out of the bowl, again using a scraper, and knead to knock the air out.

Divide the dough into 10 fingers, about 15cm/5 inches long. Place them side by side, 2cm apart on the baking sheet (they will grow together and form a batch during cooking).

Leave to prove, uncovered, for 35–45 minutes until plump and well risen. Preheat the oven to 200°C/400°F/Gas mark 6. Bake the buns for 20–25 minutes until golden. Remove the buns from the oven and transfer them to a rack without breaking up the batch. Allow to cool completely.

In the meantime, make the icing by mixing together the icing sugar and the orange juice. It is important to make the icing quite thick so it coats the back of a spoon well. Put one third of the icing in a separate bowl and colour it orange with the food dye, then spoon it into a piping bag with a very fine plain nozzle or simply into a food bag, snipping 2mm off the corner once the icing is in the bag.

Spoon icing over the buns, generously so they have a good covering. Then line up the rack so the buns are sitting vertically and, with the piping bag, pipe an orange squiggle on the surface of the buns, like piping an 'S' shape but repeatedly. Take a skewer or other pointed gadget, and draw down vertically through the squiggle of orange lines to make a feather pattern. Allow to set and they are ready.

CINNAMON ROLLS

Cinnamon is the favourite spice in the bakery, with its sweet, nutty, magnetic fragrance. Combine that with the scent of baked dough and a gooey custard centre ...

Sift 250g/9oz of the flour into a bowl, then add the yeast and caster sugar and whisk to distribute. Add the milk, vanilla and beaten egg then mix to a wet dough. Cover with a cloth and leave in a draught-free spot to rise for about 1 hour until doubled in size.

Add the rest of the flour with the salt and knead on the worktop with your hands until you have a smooth dough. Put back in the bowl and rest the dough for 5 minutes. Repeat this 'knead and rest' technique twice, then work the butter into the dough with your hands. Rest the dough again – it will be very 'active' and elastic – then fold it and place in the bowl for one further hour. Again it will double in size.

Meanwhile, make the custard. Heat the milk with the vanilla pod to boiling point. Remove from the heat and leave to infuse for 15 minutes. Scrape the seeds from the vanilla pod and add to the milk.

In a bowl, mix together the egg yolks, sugar and flour to a smooth paste. Whisk in the milk until it is all incorporated. Clean the pan, then pour the custard into it through a sieve. Heat the contents of the pan, stirring all the time, to boiling point. Whisk vigorously at this point, turning down the heat, for one minute to 'cook out' the flour so the custard texture is very creamy. Pour into a bowl, cover with greaseproof paper or cling film to prevent a skin forming, and allow to cool completely. The custard will be very thick and spreadable.

To make the buns, place the dough on to a lightly floured work surface and roll to a rectangle measuring 45x30cm/18x12 inches. Brush melted butter over the dough leaving 2cm along one short edge of the dough clear, then spread with the custard. Scatter the cinnamon evenly over the surface of the custard.

Wet the shorter unbuttered edge with water (to seal the buns) and then roll up the dough from the opposite end to make a Swiss roll measuring 30cm/12 inches.

Cut the roll into 12 pieces and place 3 rows of 4 in the baking tray – so they fit snugly. Leave to prove again until well risen.

Preheat the oven to 180°C/350°F/Gas mark 4. Bake until golden and puffed. Remove and cool in the tray. To make the glaze, boil the jam and water together in a pan until the jam melts, then sieve into a small dish (if using jelly, no sieving is required). When the buns are cool, brush with the glaze.

Makes 12

Equipment

1 roasting dish or baking tray 5cm/2 inches deep and measuring approximately 25x20cm/8x10 inches lined with a sheet of baking parchment then greased with butter

Storage

Best eaten on the day they are made, but if frozen when fresh they keep well.

Ingredients

500g/1lb 2oz strong white flour

14g/½oz dried yeast

55g/2¼oz caster sugar

265ml/9½fl oz lukewarm milk

½ teaspoon vanilla extract

1 egg, lightly beaten

7g/¼oz salt

55g/2¼oz butter, plus extra 30g/1oz, melted, for brushing

2 teaspoons ground cinnamon

For the custard:

250ml/9fl oz whole milk

1 vanilla pod, split

4 egg yolks

55g/2oz caster sugar

25g/1oz plain flour

For the glaze:

2 tablespoons apricot jam or apple jelly

2 tablespoons water

BABAS IN PINK GRAPEFRUIT SYRUP

Yeasty buns, made from a very rich dough, which are baked in small moulds then soaked in syrup. The classic version of this French baking phenomenon includes fat raisins in the dough and lots of rum in the syrup. I love it but it found no friends among the children. We devised something simpler, and more, well, babyish, so appetising sold packed in jars with syrup. This recipe can, however, be used to make the original (page 123). Serve as a pudding with whipped cream, or vanilla ice cream.

Makes about 12 buns

Equipment

12 baba moulds or a 12-hole muffin tray, lightly greased with butter

Ingredients

200ml/7fl oz cold milk

14g/½oz dried yeast

300g/10½oz plain flour

2 eggs

2 egg yolks

15g/½oz caster sugar

1 teaspoon salt

90g/3¼oz unsalted French butter, cold from the fridge, cut into small ½cm/¼ inch dice

For the syrup:

500ml/18fl oz pink grapefruit juice (freshly squeezed)

600g/1lb 5oz caster sugar

It is better to make this dough in a stand mixer. First combine the milk, yeast and one-third of the flour in the bowl, then leave for 20 minutes until bubbling and active. Beat in all the remaining ingredients of the dough, except the butter. Add this, bit by bit, with the mixer on high speed.

Once the butter has been incorporated, continue to beat for 5 minutes. The dough will be wet but elastic in appearance and texture. Cover the bowl with cling film and leave to rise either in the fridge overnight, or for 1–1½ hours in a draught-free spot.

Preheat the oven to 180°C/350°F/Gas mark 4. Stir the yeast batter to knock it down in size. Using 2 tablespoons, one to scoop and the other to shape, spoon enough dough into each baba mould or muffin recess to fill it just over half full.

Leave the babas in a draught-free spot to prove for 30–45 minutes. When they have doubled in size, bake them until puffed, crisp and golden.

In the meantime, while the dough is rising, boil the grapefruit juice and sugar together for about 5 minutes until the mixture is reduced to a syrup. Put the babas in a tall jar, and pour the syrup over the top.

CLASSIC RUM BABAS

The original recipe for babas includes raisins in the dough, and a sugar syrup with a hefty amount of rum.

Equipment
12 baba moulds or a 12-hole muffin tray, lightly greased with butter

Ingredients
1 quantity Baba dough (page 122)

150g/5½oz raisins (golden or black), soaked in 2 tablespoons rum

For the syrup:

150ml/5fl oz rum

450ml/16fl oz water

600g/1 lb 5oz caster sugar

Proceed as for the recipe on page 122, adding the raisins towards the end of the mixing process. Bake in buttered moulds. Make syrup as for Pink Grapefruit Babas.

CHRISTMAS BABAS

Bergamot are peculiar squat-shaped citrus fruit that come into season in December and taste of a combination of lemon and orange, with quite sour afternotes. They are available in continental grocers (see Suppliers, page 246). An alternative Christmas pudding.

Equipment
12 baba moulds or a 12-hole muffin tray, lightly greased with butter

Ingredients
1 quantity Baba dough (page 122)

150g/5½oz raisins (golden or black), soaked in 2 tablespoons rum

For the syrup:

150ml/5fl oz bergamot juice

450ml/16fl oz orange juice

600g/1lb 5oz caster sugar

Follow the recipe for babas and syrup on page 122.

ROSE & PISTACHIO BABAS

Babas studded with bright green pistachios, in a rose-flavoured syrup.

Equipment
12 baba moulds or a 12-hole muffin tray, lightly greased with butter

Ingredients
1 quantity Baba dough (page 122)

150g/5½oz unsalted shelled pistachios

For the syrup:

150ml/5fl oz rosewater

450ml/16fl oz water

600g/1lb 5oz caster sugar

Follow the recipe for babas and syrup on page 122.

Pastry

We are uncompromising about making pastry and using it in tarts and pies: it can only be very buttery, and rolled as thin as possible – you should be able to shine a light through it. That is our view. We steer as far as possible away from anything that might resemble manufactured tarts and pies, whose bakers (using machinery) err on the side of thick, unbreakable crusts that travel and last long on a shelf.

We are very pleased to promise that our cooked pastry is fragile, and should be eaten on the day to be at its best. This is how it should be and we have gone to some trouble to find and develop recipes that make pastry eating a marvel. We want pastry to melt in the mouth, even when it stoutly holds a filling – well, just.

For new bakers who have only just become accustomed to making bread, pastry needs a different touch. Where you put physical strength and patience into bread-making, pastry needs speed and deftness. With an amalgam of flour and butter, which melts at a lower temperature than body temperature, you can't spend too much time pummelling or handling.

Like bread, there's a bit of a hit and miss start, but confidence grows with a little practice. Mistakes are to be learned from and each time you work at it, your hands will find their own nimble ways to bring about success. It sounds odd to suggest that hands can acquire skills of their own but this is pure instinct. Recipes are only a part of it. Practice encourages intuition, and perseverance makes a good pastry cook.

Aside from a little liquid to bind pastry, this baking is all about distributing fat in wheat flour. Sometimes very thoroughly, to make a 'short' pastry, savoury or sweet, that does not expand much during cooking; or then again leaving the butter partially blended, so it expands between layers of flour and water paste to become 'puff' pastry.

Puff pastry is made in two ways: the billowing, high-rise classic 'puff' pastry, and 'rough puff', which rises, but not so dramatically. This is a more domestic pastry, one that you can easily make at home. We use rough puff pastry at the Pocket Bakery because it is more predictable, shrinks less and – we think – is the most delicious.

Not all the pastry we make is made with butter. We use a stretchy, ultra-thin pastry to envelop potatoes and fresh cheese in one of our best-loved pies, and duck fat to make hot water crust pastry, similar to that used for pork pies, which has extra crunch and flavour after slow baking.

The versatility of all these crusts makes pastry baking one of the most creative areas of cooking: from open-faced tarts, square, round and rectangular, to closed pies, plaited ribbons enclosing terrines of meat or simple, well-seasoned twists and shapes to nibble on with a drink.

The most important thing, if you are just setting out to make your first pastry, is to enjoy it. Set aside a little time; tell yourself you are a student and there is no need to be an expert yet.

MORE ABOUT PASTRY

Keep it cool. Butter melts at a lower temperature than the heat in your hands (32–35°C) so you need to handle it lightly at the rolling and shaping stage – some cooks like to rinse their hands under the cold tap ahead of handling pastry. Likewise it is always better to work in a cool room, so not when there is a Sunday roast roaring away in the oven. I have a golden rule about not making pastry when I am preparing other food, so I can concentrate. Investing in a marble board is a good idea if you intend to make pastry often as it helps to keep rolled pastry cool.

Cold, soft butter. Working with cold butter is best for keeping the pastry cool and stable. Use butter straight from the fridge, place it between two sheets of greaseproof paper and bash it with a rolling pin until it is 1cm thick. Peel back the top sheet of paper, cut into dice and use.

Judge the moisture. Like bread, the humidity in the room or moisture level in the flour will affect the moisture in the pastry. Pastry that is too dry will split and crumble as you roll it, or crack open when baked. Pastry that is too wet will take longer to cook and not crisp up under a filled tart. It is also very hard to handle, especially in the case of flaky pastry. To test the moisture in raw pastry just after it has been made, pinch it between finger and thumb. It should not crumble or break apart (too dry), or feel too soft so your digits meet (too wet) but feel smooth and malleable with some resistance. Add a little water (if dry) or flour (if wet), lightly kneading it into the dough.

Roll it evenly. It's too easy to make the mistake of rolling pastry unevenly, despite a ram-rod straight rolling pin and flat board. Maybe it is because all of us have a stronger side to our bodies, but too often a rolled sheet of pastry can appear wedge-shaped, like the Isle of Wight! Just remember to use an even amount of power with both hands when rolling.

Fix it. When the perfect round of pastry you just made beautifully splits as you put it in a tin, or a hole appears, just take another piece, finger-paint it with a little water and patch it up. What seems like a real catastrophe is often not the end. Sometimes a pie crust will fall into the pie contents – it is a sight to make you sob. It usually happens because the pie filling was warm when the pastry was laid on, or because the pastry was too wet, but don't panic or try to fix it. Shut the oven door and leave it. It will crisp up – if it has the same high butter content of the recipes in this chapter.

Soggy bottoms. A phrase now so notorious we must address it. This is when the pastry base of a filled tart (or pie) does not cook through and, when the tart is cut, there seems to be a layer of cardboard under the tart contents. If the pastry is not rolled thin enough, does not contain a generous quantity of butter and/or is not baked for the right length of time – the base will be soggy. Since the Pocket Bakery's pastry recipes are very richly buttery, and we will be on at you to roll it thin, soggy bottoms are easily avoidable.

Thin rolling. Thinly rolled pastry is stronger than you think, easier to handle, but most of all nicer to bite than a thick dry crust. Even hot water crust (pork pie pastry) need not be thick and solid. We go by the principle that we'd prefer a fragile pie to crack or a tart rim to chip than cooked pastry that can be dropped without breaking. But what defines 'thin'? Rolling out thin means to ¼cm, that's ⅒ of an inch. Please trust us – the shortcrust recipe in this book is very resilient, and if the rough puff is kept cool enough and not too wet, it is easy to roll it this thin.

Baking 'blind'. This is the term we use when making a pastry case. After the tart case has been lined, it must then be baked with a weight inside it to prevent the pastry base from rising into a dome. If this happens, you will not be able to fill the tart properly. Once the pastry is pressed into the tin, line it with a circle of baking parchment then fill with dried beans. After baking, the beans can be removed and stored for reuse.

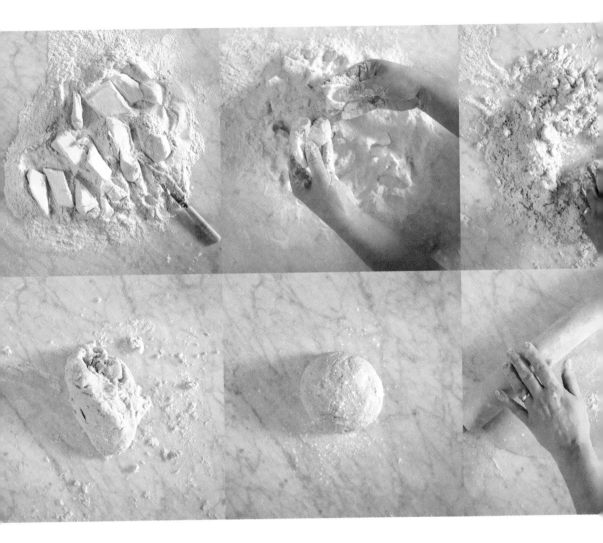

SHORTCRUST PASTRY

Pastry for savoury tarts and pies that can be rolled very thinly, is easy to handle and will not shrink or expand during cooking except to become slightly flaky. We recommend plain flour and standard unsalted butter for savoury shortcrust pastry. If you use Italian fine-milled '00' flour, you will be able to roll it even thinner, which can be an advantage for making lightweight individual pies, such as Christmas mince pies.

Makes approximately 700g/1½lb pastry, enough for at least 2 tarts, to cover 2 pies, to make 24 mince pies or for 8 pasties

....

Ingredients

1 teaspoon **salt**

375g/13oz **plain flour**, plus extra for dusting

250g /9oz diced **butter**

125–150ml/4–5 fl oz ice-cold **water**

....

Sieve the salt and flour together in a large bowl, add the butter and mix to a breadcrumb stage. This can be done in a stand mixer using the dough hook, or in a food processor. Add the water, and mix until it comes together as a dough.

At this stage pinch a little bit of the dough between thumb and index finger. It should not crumble or break apart (too dry), or feel too soft so your digits meet (too wet), but feel smooth and malleable with some resistance. Add a little water (if dry) or flour (if wet), lightly kneading it into the dough.

Take the dough out of the mixing bowl and knead on a very lightly floured worktop until it is smooth. Form into an oblong tablet (easier when it comes to dividing for use later), wrap in cling film and rest in the fridge for at least 20 minutes before using. It will store in the fridge for 24 hours, or in the freezer for up to 2 weeks if frozen when very fresh.

Rolling the pastry into a circle

Remove the pastry from the fridge and leave for 30 minutes to soften slightly. Dust the worktop with flour, cut the quantity you need to make the tart (see quantities, above) and place it on the worktop. Tap the pastry all over the surface with the rolling pin to flatten it a little, then begin to roll, making one swift, even movement back and forth. So you end up with an even circle, turn the pastry 30 degrees and roll back and forth once again. Check there is enough flour dusted under the pastry and add a little more if it is beginning to stick. Continue to roll in this way until you have a circle the size of a dinner plate. It will become too difficult to turn the pastry each time from now on, so (checking it is not sticking) adjust the angle you roll to roll it to ¼cm/1/10 inch thick, in an almost perfect circle.

BLIND-BAKING

Preheat the oven to 180°C/350°F/Gas mark 4. You do not need to butter the tart tin. Pick up the pastry by wrapping it around the rolling pin then drape it loosely across the tin. Ease the pastry down the sides making sure it is well tucked into the corners. Press it up against the sides and allow the extra to hang over the top edge as it will be trimmed after baking.

Prick the base of the pastry a few times, to prevent the base lifting during cooking. You only need to do this with savoury shortcrust pastry; sweet pastry is heavier and richer, and although it needs to be blind-baked, it tends not to bubble up as much. Place a sheet of baking parchment inside the tart and more than half fill with dried haricot beans (or rice or ceramic baking beans).

Bake for about 20 minutes, until the pastry is dry under the beans, but not brown. Take the tart out of the oven and turn the temperature down to 170°C/Gas mark 3, remove the paper lining and beans, and return to the oven for 5 minutes to crisp the pastry base a little more.

The pastry case is now ready to use. If any cracks appear during cooking, patch them with spare pastry, stuck on with water. Bake for 5 minutes to secure the patches. If you are making a pastry case with a liquid mixture, such as beaten eggs and milk for a cheese tart or lemon cream for a lemon tart, brush the inside of the blind-baked pastry case with beaten egg and return to the oven to harden.

This pastry case can be frozen in advance of being used, and will keep in an airtight container for 3 days.

HOT WATER CRUST PASTRY

The pastry used to make cold meat pies, such as pork pies, is easy to make, but when using it, it is important to have the confidence to use it sparingly so the base, sides and lid of the pie will not be thick. This pastry should be cooked until it is dark and crunchy, but too thick a crust makes it unpleasant to eat. I make it with duck fat, inspired by baker Richard Bertinet, but it is more common to use lard. Duck fat gives hot water crust extra flavour, and wonderful colour.

Most pies made with this pastry are cooked in high-sided moulds: either muffin trays, as for the duck and pork hand pies on page 152, or in pretty hinged terrine moulds. I know a baker who uses half-size former baked beans cans to make individual pork pies.

Makes enough for one 18cm/7-inch pie with lid or 8 individual pies

••

Ingredients

450g plain flour

1 egg, lightly beaten

1 egg yolk

175g/6oz duck fat, or lard, melted and kept warm

175ml/6fl oz boiling water

1 teaspoon salt

1 teaspoon icing sugar

To glaze:

1 egg, beaten with 1 tablespoon water and 1 pinch salt

Have the filling ready before making the pastry, or make the filling while the pastry rests in the fridge.

Put the flour in a large bowl and stir in the egg and yolk. Add the duck fat and water with the salt and icing sugar, then mix until you have a soft dough. Roll it out lightly on a floured worktop, then fold into 3. Wrap in cling film or greaseproof paper and refrigerate for 1 hour or until firm. The pastry is now ready to use.

ROUGH PUFF PASTRY

Pastry with a very high butter content, though the butter is not completely blended with the flour as it is for shortcrust pastry. As a result it rises during cooking, into crisp buttery layers, up to an inch high. It is best baked fully for greater flavour, so I tend to allow it to bake to a deep gold.

We advise you to stick exactly to the amount of water in this pastry. You will think, when first mixing, that it is too dry. Adding more, however, will make the pastry soft and impossible to handle or roll without sticking to the pin and the worktop. We recommend using plain white flour and either British or French unsalted butter.

The pastry goes through three 'rolling and folding' stages before it is ready to use. During this time, the dry bits in the dough will be absorbed into the dough.

It may seem complicated at first, and the end result may look a bit rough, hence the name, but even if you have made a few mistakes – excepting adding extra water, which is forbidden – it will rise and taste delicious to a great extent.

Makes 1kg pastry/2¼ lb, enough for 3 tarts of 25x35cm/10x14-inch or 12 individual tarts. We find it is better to make a larger amount and freeze what we do not use, saving time because it is made in stages.

Ingredients

500g/1lb 2oz **butter**

500g/1lb 2oz **plain flour**, plus extra for dusting

250ml/9oz ice-cold **water**

Put the butter between two sheets of greaseproof paper and tap hard with a rolling pin to soften. Put all the flour in a heap on the work surface, make a well in the centre and add the butter. Use your fingers (rinsed under cold tap and dried) to partially rub the butter into the flour, just to flatten the pieces, keeping them large, not to break them up further at this stage.

Add the water and form into a dry-ish dough; it will look crusty at the edges and there will be loose flour but do not try to incorporate it at this stage. Wrap the piece of dough in greaseproof paper and put in the fridge for 15 minutes.

Clean the work surface using a dough scraper and dust it with a little flour. Take the dough from the fridge and unwrap it. Swiftly roll it into a rectangle, about 20x40cm/8x16 inches. Fold it into three, like a letter (bring one third to the centre, then bring over the opposite third of pastry to lie on top of the fold). Tap it with a rolling pin, turn it 90 degrees, then roll out again to 20x40cm making sure that it is not sticking and there is enough flour on the worktop.

Repeat this process: fold, tap with the rolling pin, then wrap and refrigerate again for 30 minutes. The pastry should by now have absorbed the dry and floury bits. Marbled lumps of butter will be visible inside the dough. Occasionally a lump of butter breaks through – just dust the area with flour if this happens.

Repeat the rolling, folding and tapping twice more, and refrigerate for at least 30 minutes before using the pastry.

Rolling the pastry – for a fruit or savoury tart
You will need some egg glaze – beat together 1 egg, 1 tablespoon water, pinch salt.

Preheat the oven to 220°C/425°F/Gas mark 7 and put the baking sheet you will be using in the oven. Cut the quantity of pastry you need. Dust the worktop with flour and roll it out to a thickness of ¼cm/1/10 inch. Pick it up, rolling it on to a well-floured rolling pin, then unroll it on to a sheet of baking parchment. This will be easily slipped on to the preheated baking sheet and ensures the base of the tart will be crisp.

Spread or arrange the filling on to the pastry leaving a border of about 2cm/¾ inch; brush the edges with egg wash and bake for 15–25 minutes until the pastry edges are golden. Check that the base is cooked by gently lifting a corner of the tart and looking underneath. If it is not quite cooked, give the tart a few more minutes, turning the oven down so you do not burn the edges.

SWEET PASTRY

Sunny, golden tart pastry, with a rich flavour that is used to make tarts, and a world away from that pale powdery bought type that sticks to the roof of the mouth. This pastry can and should be rolled very thin, and bakes to a crisp – I am not satisfied unless it is snappy as a biscuit.

It is not difficult to make but you need patience to line a tart tin with this pastry because it has little malleability. It almost certainly will split and break on the first attempts, but do not worry. Just patch it and the result will look great.

Use it to line tins for fruit tarts and baked tarts (e.g. Classic lemon tart, page 158).

Makes enough for 2 large tarts, 20cm in diameter, 4cm deep, or 24 x 8cm tartlets, 2cm deep

· ·

Ingredients

350g/12oz **plain white flour**, plus extra for dusting

Pinch **salt**

125g/4½oz cold **butter**

125g/4½oz **sugar**

2 eggs plus 1 **egg yolk**

Put the flour and salt into a bowl. Take the butter from the fridge, put it between two pieces of greaseproof paper and bash it firmly with a rolling pin until it is 1cm/½ inch thick, pliable but still cold.

Put the butter into the bowl with the flour and tear it into pieces. Try to keep the butter coated with flour so it doesn't stick. Gently flake the butter into the flour, with your fingers, rubbing lightly, then delving back into the mixture to lift and rub.

Stop flaking when the pieces of butter are the size of your little fingernail. Scatter the sugar over. Tip the eggs and extra yolk into the flour and mix everything together thoroughly with a spoon until you have a lumpy dough.

Turn the dough out on to the worktop then squeeze with your hand and push it with your knuckles until it's a heavy smooth paste. Do not over-work the dough – the high butter and egg content means it could become greasy. Form the dough into an oblong, wrap it in cling film and leave to rest in the fridge for 30 minutes.

Rolling sweet pastry
Make sure, when rolling, that the worktop is well dusted with flour and, as you roll it, check that it is not sticking. If it does, add more flour.

Put the pastry on the floured worktop and tap with a rolling pin to flatten it a little. To form

a circle of pastry, use the rolling pin to roll it backward and forwards once, then turn the disc of pastry 30 degrees. Roll back and forth again then turn again. Repeat this action several times, checking regularly that there is enough flour under the pastry and on the rolling pin to prevent sticking. At some point the pastry will be too thin to turn, so just adjust the direction you roll, mindful that is not sticking.

Lining a tart case

Once the pastry is ¼cm/⅒-inch thick (or a little more if you are not confident), it must be very carefully picked up. Roll it on to the pin, keeping the rolling pin very close to it. Do not worry if it splits; this pastry repairs easily once in the tin. Unroll it over the tin, quickly tucking it into the tin as you go with your other hand.

Press the pastry into the corners of the tin, and against the sides. Allow it to fall over the top edge but do not trim, this can be done after cooking. Repair any holes or cracks with spare pastry, pressing it with your fingers. Do not prick with a fork – this pastry is heavy and will not bubble up much during blind-baking. Also, the filling might escape. Put the tart case in the fridge for 20 minutes.

Preheat the oven to 180°C/350°F/Gas mark 4. Line the tin with baking parchment and then fill with dry rice, beans or baking beans. Bake for 15 minutes, remove from the oven, take out the paper and beans, brush the inside with beaten egg to seal it and bake for another 5 minutes to crisp the base – turn the oven down by 10°C so the edges will not overcook.

Tip

Some bakers, when making individual tarts, do not roll the pastry and line the tins but press a piece of pastry into the tin until it is the right thickness. Make sure to have cool hands to do this. Run them under the cold tap and dry them often or keep a bowl of iced water nearby.

OLIVE OIL PASTRY

This is based on pastry used in Italian baking, but is also similar to strudel paste in that it is a resilient pastry that can be stretched to make it paper-thin. The extraordinary thing about this fragile-looking, ultra-thin crust that one could shine a light through, is that it is not hard to handle and it cooks to a crisp without bursting its banks (though I admit a little delicious juice from the pie contents may seep from under it).

We use this pastry to make large pies filled with potato, woody herbs and fresh cheese – alternating the ingredients to include crisp chunks of smoked bacon, blue cheeses, roasted tomatoes or seasonal ingredients like wild garlic.

You must use fine-milled Italian '00' flour (usually used to make pasta), or the pastry will be coarse-textured, and also be aware that the quantity of water you need to add depends on the dryness of the flour. The pastry, once made, should be a little tacky but not stick to the mixing bowl.

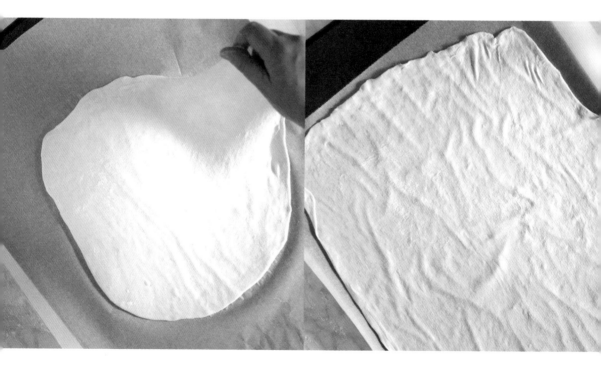

Makes approximately 220g/8oz pastry, enough for one 35cm/14-inch pie

．．

Ingredients

150g/5½oz **Italian '00' white flour**, plus extra for dusting

½ teaspoon **salt**

1½ tablespoons **olive oil**

75–100ml/2½–3 ½fl oz iced **water**

．．

Put the flour and salt into a mixing bowl, or stand mixer with dough hook attached, and mix in the olive oil. Add 75ml/2½fl oz of the water and mix – adding more water until you have a soft dough that is not sticking to the mixing bowl, but is a little tacky to touch.

Take the dough out of the mixing bowl and knead until completely smooth on a lightly floured worktop. It will feel elastic and soft. Wrap the dough in cling film and leave to rest in the fridge for 30 minutes. This dough can be made 24 hours in advance of being used.

To roll and stretch the dough

Take the dough from the fridge and dust the worktop with a little flour. Roll the dough into a disc, about the size of a dessert plate. Leave for 2 minutes for it to relax (making sure it is not sticking to the worktop – you may need more flour). Roll again very thin, until it is the size of a dinner plate and about ¼cm/1/10-inch thick.

Place the disc of dough on a lightly floured baking sheet. Gently pull at the edge, holding the dough lightly in floured fingers, stretching at one point and moving around the whole circumference of the dough. The circle will expand in size until the dough covers the whole of the baking sheet and more.

You will find that if you work patiently and slowly, and allow the dough to rest between stretching from time to time, it will allow you to stretch it paper-thin. If little tears appear, it does not matter. You will be surprised how this dough does not change shape during cooking and how the tears do not get bigger. When the dough is about 45cm/18 inches across, it is ready to fill.

Note

Once the pastry is stretched it must be used immediately or it will begin to dry out and become unworkable.

CHEESE & HAM HOCK TART

A hot cheese tart, souffléd as it comes out of the oven and slightly runny inside, bordered by crisp shortcrust pastry still endures as a favourite. It is even better when speckled with chunks of ham hock, which is an inexpensive cured cut, but you can substitute other things, like undyed smoked haddock, or chard. Use diced ham if you prefer, and you can also substitute other types of cheese: Gruyère, Lancashire cheese, or try a modern British cheese like Ogleshield or the Irish cheese, St Gall.

Makes a 20cm/8-inch tart,
serving 4–6

. . . .

Equipment
20cm/8-inch tart tin, 4cm/1 ½
inches deep, with a loose base,
placed on a baking sheet

. . . .

Ingredients
1 ham hock, soaked in cold water
for several hours – yielding
250–300g lean meat

1 star anise

1 bay leaf

Flour, for dusting

Half quantity Shortcrust Pastry
(page 133)

115g/4oz grated mature
Cheddar cheese

2 eggs

2 egg yolks

300ml/10fl oz double cream

A few gratings of nutmeg

Salt and black pepper

Put the ham hock in a pan, add the anise and bay leaf; cover with water and bring to the boil. Turn the heat down so the pan is simmering and cook for 2 hours until the meat is falling off the bone. Drain, then, when cool enough, separate the meat from the bone, fat and other tissue and set it aside. Discard the bay and anise.

Put the pastry on a worktop dusted with flour. Tap it with a rolling pin to flatten it a little. Roll it back and forth once, turn the pastry disc 30 degrees and roll backwards and forwards once more. Continue – checking there is enough flour underneath and the pastry is not sticking – until you have a disc the size of a plate. Stop turning the pastry after a bit and continue to roll, changing the direction often, until the pastry is ¼cm/1/10-inch thick and more than 30cm/12-inches across.

Pick up the pastry by rolling it on to the pin, and lay it over the tart tin. Fit it into the tin, pushing it into the corners and up against the sides. Allow the pastry to fall over the edges – do not trim it at this stage. Prick the base with a fork in 4 places. Put it in the fridge for 20 minutes.

Preheat the oven to 190°C/375°F/Gas mark 5. Line the pastry case with baking paper and place it on the baking sheet. Fill to half the depth of the tin with dried beans or rice, or baking beans. Bake for 15 minutes, then remove the paper and beans and bake for another 5 minutes to crisp the base – turn the oven down by 10°C so the edges will not overcook.

Scatter the ham hock meat over the base of the tart, followed by the cheese. Beat together the eggs, egg yolks and cream, and season with the nutmeg, salt and pepper. Pour this mixture carefully into the tin – up to about ½cm/¼ inch from the top of the tin.

Bake the tart for 25–30 minutes, until golden and risen. Trim the top edge of the tart with a very sharp knife or fine serrated knife. Serve immediately, or enjoy this tart at room temperature. You can also reheat it gently at 170°C/325°F/Gas mark 3.

WATERCRESS & FRESH CHEESE TART

One of the many beauties of watercress is that it retains its lovely lawn-green colour during cooking – matched with a fresh cheese, this is a lighter tart for summer supper and picnics.

Serves 4–6

....

Equipment

20cm/8-inch tart tin, 4cm/1 ½ inches deep, with a loose base, placed on a baking sheet

....

Ingredients

Flour, for dusting

Half quantity Shortcrust Pastry (page 133)

1 bunch of watercress, main stalks removed, roughly chopped

115g/4oz mature fresh curd cheese or buffalo ricotta

2 eggs

2 egg yolks

300ml/10fl oz double cream

A few gratings of nutmeg

Salt and black pepper

2 tablespoons grated Grana Padano, or Parmesan cheese, or mature Cheddar

To serve:

more watercress leaves, dressed with a small amount of olive oil

Put the pastry on a worktop dusted with flour. Tap it with a rolling pin to flatten it a little. Roll it back and forth once, turn the pastry disc 30 degrees and roll backwards and forwards once more. Continue – checking there is enough flour and the pastry is not sticking – until you have a disc the size of a plate. Stop turning the pastry after a bit and continue to roll, changing the direction, until the pastry is ¼cm/1/10-inch thick and more than 30cm/12 inches across.

Pick up the pastry by rolling it on to the pin, and lay it over the tart tin. Fit it into the tin, pushing it into the corners and up against the sides. Allow the pastry to fall over the edges – do not trim it at this stage. Prick the base with a fork in 4 places. Put it in the fridge for 20 minutes.

Preheat the oven to 190°C/375°F/Gas mark 5. Line the tin with baking paper and place on the baking sheet. Half fill with dried beans or rice, or baking beans. Bake for 15 minutes, then remove the paper and beans and bake for another 5 minutes to crisp the base – turn the oven down by 10°C so the edges will not overcook.

Scatter the chopped watercress over the base of the tart, then add the cheese by the teaspoon, spacing lumps of it evenly around. Beat together the eggs, egg yolks and cream, and season with the nutmeg, salt and pepper. Pour this mixture carefully into the tin – up to about ½cm/¼ inch from the top of the tin.

Bake the tart for 25–30 minutes, until golden and risen. Trim the top edge of the tart with a very sharp knife or fine serrated knife. Serve hot, or at room temperature when it is nice to heap a little watercress salad on to the surface.

TOMATO TART
WITH ANCHOVIES

A reminder of walks through Antibes market with my grand-mother who lived near the town for 50 years and loved the local food. There would always be bakers at the market, cutting pieces from huge tarts cooked in rectangular tins, spread with sweet cooked onion (pissaladière) or puréed tomato, olives and strips of anchovy. These tarts are often made with yeast dough, but my favourites have a pastry base.

This is a tart we make often for the bakery, using our rough puff pastry. We make another version with thin slices of mozzarella cheese in place of the anchovies, a pastry pizza popular – I need hardly add – with children. Use good quality Italian canned tomatoes; the San Marzano type is best if you can find them.

Put all the ingredients for the cooked tomato in a pan, bring to the boil and cook for 10 minutes. Purée in a blender/food processor, or put through a food mill (mouli).

Preheat the oven to 220°C/425°F/Gas mark 7 and put the baking sheet you will be using in the oven. Dust the worktop with flour and roll the pastry out to ¼cm/⅒-inch thickness. Pick it up, rolling it on to a well-floured rolling pin, then unroll it on to a sheet of baking parchment. This will be easily slipped on to the preheated baking sheet and ensures the base of the tart will be crisp.

Spread the cooked tomato on to the pastry leaving a border of about 2cm/¾ inch; place the anchovies all over the surface, plus the olives, all evenly spaced.

Brush the edges with egg wash and bake for 15–25 minutes until the pastry edges are golden. Check that the base is cooked by gently lifting a corner of the tart and looking underneath. If not quite cooked, give the tart a few more minutes, turning the oven down so you do not burn the edges.

Eat hot from the oven, or at room temperature. This tart reheats very nicely.

Serves 4–6

Equipment

1 baking sheet measuring approximately 25x40cm/10x15 inches

Ingredients

For the cooked tomato:

400g/14oz tin chopped tomatoes

1 garlic clove, crushed

4 basil leaves

4 tablespoons olive oil

For the tart:

Flour, for dusting

300g Rough Puff Pastry (pages 136–137)

12 anchovies, cut lengthways in 2

12 black olives (preferably Niçoise), halved and stoned

To glaze:

1 egg, beaten with 1 tablespoon water and 1 pinch salt

CHICKEN, LEEK & TARRAGON PIE

Heavenly partnerships in cooking are hard to improve upon, and this pie, which we have eaten as a family for many years with buttered baked potatoes, brings together the amazing trinity of tender simmered chicken, tarragon and leeks. It is a pie with only a lid of pastry, one of the easiest to make, and I encourage you to use all of the chicken, including the darker meat from the legs. You can also use leftover roast chicken in this recipe.

Remember to make sure the filling is cool before putting the crust on the pie – it is a good idea to make the white sauce and poach the chicken in advance, then the pie can be assembled quickly later in the day.

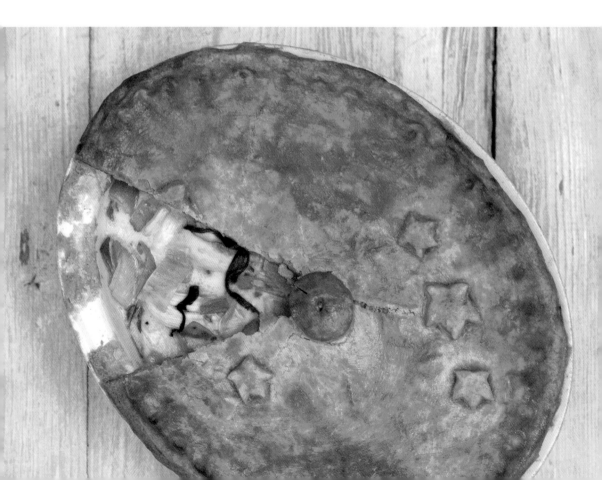

Put the whole chicken in a large casserole with all the other poaching ingredients and cover with water. Bring to the boil, then turn the heat down so the pot simmers. Cook for 1 hour and 15 minutes until the meat comes easily away from the bone. Be careful not to cook it so long that the meat is in threads. Lift the bird out of the pot and allow it to cool. Save the stock for the sauce, passing it through a sieve. Pull all the meat from the carcass. Don't forget the wing meat and the two oysters on the underside close to the wing joints. Set the meat to one side.

Next make the sauce. Heat the stock to boiling point in a saucepan, then remove from the heat and pour into a jug. Melt the butter in the same pan, add the flour and cook over a medium heat until the mixture looks pale and sandy.

Add the stock, whisking, then bring to the boil, stirring slowly. As the sauce comes to the boil it will thicken. When it boils, stop stirring, turn down the heat and allow to cook for 2 minutes to get rid of the floury taste. Add the cream and tarragon, stir, season with salt and pepper to taste and remove from the heat. Pour it into the pie dish (put a pie chimney or upturned egg cup in the centre of the dish to support the pastry) and add the chicken meat.

Melt the butter in a pan and add the leeks. Stir-fry for a few moments for the leeks to 'green up' and soften a little. Add the leeks to the pie dish and allow the contents of the dish to cool.

Preheat the oven to 190°C/375°F/Gas mark 5. Roll out the shortcrust pastry on a floured worktop into an oval about 5cm/2 inches larger than the pie dish. Brush the edges of the pie dish with egg glaze. Cut a 3cm/1-inch strip from around the pastry oval and stick it to the pie dish rim. Lift the pie covering with a rolling pin and unroll it over the pie. Press down the edges, using your fingers, so they are well welded to the strip of pastry around the rim. Allow any extra pie pastry to droop over the edges.

Cut a small circle the size of a 50p piece from the spare pastry. Stick it, with egg glaze, on the centre of the pie crust, over the chimney, and then pierce a hole in the centre of it with the point of a knife. This is so that steam can escape from the pie during cooking. You can use the other spare pastry to cut in shapes to decorate the pie, if you wish, sticking the decorations on with egg glaze.

Refrigerate the uncooked pie for about 15 minutes before baking (or up to 24 hours). Brush the whole surface with egg glaze. Bake the pie for 30–40 minutes until the pie crust is golden and burnished, and the contents can be heard bubbling underneath. Serve immediately.

Serves 4–6

Equipment

Pie dish measuring 25cm/10 inches across

Ingredients

For the poached chicken:

1 large chicken

1 bay leaf

2 carrots, split in half

1 onion, split in half

1 celery stick, roughly chopped

A few gratings of nutmeg

1 bay leaf

For the sauce:

600ml/1 pint stock from the poached chicken

30g/1oz butter

1 heaped tablespoon plain flour

150ml double cream

Leaves from 2 sprigs of tarragon

Salt and pepper

For the leeks:

1 nut of butter

2 leeks, split, cut into 2cm/¾-inch chunks and washed

For the pastry:

Half quantity Shortcrust Pastry (page 133)

To glaze:

1 egg, beaten with 1 tablespoon water and 1 pinch salt

DUCK & PORK HAND PIES

So called because one will fit in the hand. I love these domed individual pies mostly for the crunchy pastry – hot water crust, made with duck fat, which can be eaten hot or cold. You can omit the pork or use only duck meat making up the total meat weight, if you like.

Makes 4

....

Equipment

4 large individual pie tins or foil containers, measuring about 10cm/4 inches

....

Ingredients

For the filling:

25g/1oz butter

100g/3½oz chopped pancetta

6 small shallots, finely chopped (about 3 tablespoons)

1 teaspoon dried oregano

1 apple, peeled, cored and grated

350g/12oz minced pork shoulder

350g/12oz minced duck leg meat or breast, including fat

2 tablespoons cider brandy

1 teaspoon salt

1 teaspoon ground white pepper

For the pastry:

1 quantity Hot Water Crust (page 135), which can be made up to 24 hours earlier and stored in the fridge, wrapped in cling film

To glaze:

1 egg, beaten with 1 tablespoon water and 1 pinch salt

Put the butter in a frying pan and melt it over a medium heat. Add the pancetta, then the chopped shallots and oregano. Cook, stirring, until lightly browned. Add the apple, then cook for a further minute. Remove from the heat and allow to cool. Put in a bowl and mix with the meat, brandy, salt and white pepper.

Preheat the oven to 180°C/350°F/Gas mark 4. To make the pies, cut the pastry in two: one-third for the lids and two-thirds for the casings. Roll out the larger piece to ½cm/¼-inch thick. Cut 4 circles 2cm/¾ inch larger than the pie tins. Line the tins, leaving an overhang. Fill with the pork and duck mixture, heaping it in a dome in the centre. Roll out the smaller piece to the same thickness and cut 4 circles large enough to cover the pies.

Brush the edges with water, then place the second piece of pastry loosely on top. Pinch the edges together, trim them, then crimp them with your fingers. It is important not to make the pie too tight or it will ooze juice during cooking and be difficult to get out of the tin.

Make a hole in the centre of the pie so steam can escape during cooking. Brush with egg glaze, then bake the pies for 45 minutes until they are deep golden brown. Brush with a little more glaze 5 minutes before the end of cooking. Eat while still warm. These pies reheat well.

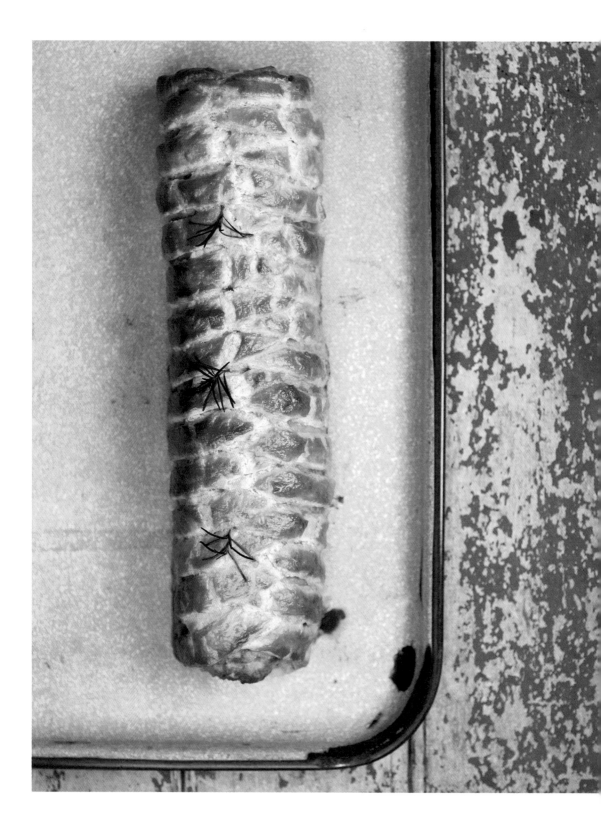

SAUSAGE PLAIT WITH PANCETTA & FENNEL SEEDS

This is a sort of giant slicing sausage roll with rough puff pastry woven around it; very good hot and freshly cooked, but also a decorative and enjoyable picnic basket or cold lunch piece. Use good quality naturally reared pork, to prevent a watery filling.

Preheat the oven to 190°C/375°F/Gas mark 5. Put the sausage meat and all the filling ingredients in a bowl and mix well with your hands. Place a sheet of baking parchment on the table and heap the forcemeat mixture on to it. Make a large sausage, about 9cm/3½ inches in diameter, and roll it in the baking paper.

Lightly flour the worktop and roll out the rough puff pastry thinly – about 4mm/¼-inch thick. Make sure, as you roll it, that it is not sticking to the worktop – add more flour under the pastry sheet if necessary. Trim it to make a rectangle measuring 25x40cm.

Pick up the pastry sheet, rolling it on to a floured rolling pin, and unroll it on to the baking sheet. Now lay the pancetta slices on top of it, side by side going down the length of the pastry sheet. Lift the sausage wrapped in paper and unroll it out of the paper so it sits lengthways in the centre of the pastry sheet.

Take a sharp knife and cut the borders of the pastry horizontal to the sausage, into ribbons, each 2cm/½-inch wide. Starting at one end, bring the first two ribbons either side of the sausage up to meet in the centre. Lay one down on the sausage and let the other one cross over it. Continue like this until the whole sausage has the pastry woven around it.

Tuck the rosemary sprigs under the ribbons of the plait in three places. Then brush the whole thing with egg glaze. Refrigerate for 15 minutes to firm up the pastry, then bake for 45 minutes, until golden. Insert a skewer into the middle of the sausage plait – if it comes out very hot, the plait is cooked. If it is warm but not hot, give the plait more time, but turn down the oven. Serve hot or cold. This plait reheats well.

Serves 6–8

Equipment

Baking sheet measuring 25x40cm/10x15 inches, lightly greased with butter, then well dusted with flour

Ingredients

For the filling:

1kg/2¼lb **sausage meat**

1 tablespoon **Madeira** or sherry

1 teaspoon **fennel seeds**

Leaves from 2 sprigs **rosemary**

Salt and **pepper**

½ teaspoon grated **nutmeg**

1 **egg**, beaten

200g/7oz fresh **breadcrumbs**

For the pastry:

Half quantity **Rough Puff Pastry** (pages 136–137)

10 thin slices **pancetta**

To finish and glaze:

3 sprigs **rosemary**

1 **egg**, beaten with 1 tablespoon **water** and 1 pinch **salt**

PLEATED PIE WITH POTATO, WOODY HERBS & FRESH CHEESE

The pastry used in this pie breaks all the rules. Made with olive oil and finely milled pasta flour, it is not rolled but stretched around the filling of creamy potato, herbs and fresh cheese. The intricate pleating of this transparently thin dough looks tricky but you will be surprised how sturdy and malleable it is. It also stays strong in cooking – if you tear it, the filling stays put.

Makes one large pie measuring 20–25cm, serving 8 as a main or 12 as a side dish

Equipment
Baking sheet measuring 25x40cm/10x15 inches, lined with baking parchment

Ingredients
1.6kg/3lb 6oz (10–12 medium-sized) floury potatoes, Romano or Desiree

200ml/7fl oz double cream

100g/3½oz grated strong cheese: Cheddar, Parmesan or other mature type

2 eggs

Salt

4 tablespoons olive oil, plus a little more for the surface of the pie

Leaves from 1 sprig rosemary

Leaves from 2 sprigs sage

Leaves from 2 sprigs thyme

2 garlic cloves, chopped

1 quantity Olive Oil Pastry (pages 140–141)

250g buffalo ricotta or other fresh creamy cheese

Boil the potatoes in their skins until tender in the centre. Drain then peel using rubber gloves – they are easier to peel when hot. Place in a bowl and mash roughly. Beat in the cream, grated cheese and eggs, then add salt to taste.

In a small pan, heat the olive oil over a medium heat and add the herb leaves and garlic. Allow the olive oil to simmer for a minute or two but do not brown the herbs and garlic.

Preheat the oven to 200°C/400°F/Gas mark 6. Roll and stretch the dough as described on page 141, then spoon the mashed potato on to the stretched pastry, in a round covering an area 30cm/12 inches across. Spoon over the ricotta cheese in little heaps, evenly spaced, then pour the herb and garlic oil over the top.

Very gently, pick up the edges of the dough and pull it up and over towards the centre, pleating it as you work. Do not worry if it tears – you can pinch it together again – but even so, this pastry will not tear further as it bakes. Once the edges are all gathered at the centre of the pie, trim off any that are thicker than 1mm as they will be tough once baked.

Drip some more olive oil on to the surface, then bake until pale gold and crisp – about 25–30 minutes. Do not allow it to become too dark. The pie can be stored in the fridge after baking for 24 hours and reheats well. It is lovely eaten as a main course, hot or lukewarm, or with boiled ham or grilled sausages.

Variations

It is easy to change the fillings for olive oil pastry pies. We tend to add any cheese that needs eating, and have experimented with cured meat. Try any one of the following:

- Fried chorizo sausage, roasted pepper and fresh goat's cheese

- Crisp bacon, sage and sautéed chicory

- Roasted tomato, basil and mozzarella

- Blue cheese, Swiss chard and thyme – in this instance, replace the mashed potato with 1.3kg/3lb boiled new potatoes, sliced

CLASSIC LEMON TART WITH FRESH LEMON FILAMENTS

A not-to-be-ignored classic; it seems only yesterday that lemon tarts began turning up on menus, yet it must have been 25 years ago. The best are those with the most powerful lemon flavour, and – to perhaps labour an often-made point made in this pastry chapter – are enclosed in a pastry shell as translucent as bone china, and just as precious. We like to place a few filaments of fresh lemon on top to season the tart with sharpness.

Serves 6–8

....

Equipment

25cm/10 inch **tart tin**, 4cm deep, with a loose base, placed on a baking sheet

A **butane blowtorch** (optional)

....

Ingredients

Flour, for dusting

300g/10 ½oz **Sweet Pastry** (pages 138–139), at room temperature

1 **egg**, beaten

For the filling:

6 **eggs**

300g/10½oz **caster sugar**

300ml/½ pint freshly squeezed **lemon juice**

Zest of 4 lemons

185g/6¼oz **double cream**

To seal the tart case:

1 **egg** beaten with a few grains of **salt**

To serve:

Icing sugar

Whole filaments (pulp of the lemon), carefully cut out of lemon segments, left on a cloth to dry

First roll the pastry and line the tart tin. Make sure, when rolling, that the worktop is well dusted with flour and, as you roll it thin, check that it is not sticking. If it does, add more flour.

Put the pastry on the floured worktop and tap with a rolling pin to flatten it a little. Roll the pin backwards and forwards over the pastry once, then turn the disc 30 degrees. Roll back and forth again then turn again. Repeat this action several times, checking regularly that there is enough flour under the pastry and on the rolling pin to prevent sticking. At some point the pastry will be too thin to turn, so just adjust the direction you roll, checking that it is not sticking.

Once the pastry is ¼cm/1⁄10-inch thick (or a little more if you are not confident), it must be very carefully picked up. Roll it on to the pin, keeping the rolling pin very close to it. Do not worry if there is any splitting; this pastry repairs easily once in the tin. Unroll it over the tin, quickly tucking it into the tin with your other hand as you go.

Press the pastry into the corners of the tin, and against the sides. Allow it to fall over the top edge but do not trim; this can be done after cooking. Repair any holes or cracks with spare pastry, pressing it with your fingers. Do not prick with a fork, or the filling might escape. Put the tart case in the fridge for 20 minutes.

Preheat the oven to 180°C/350°F/Gas mark 4. Line the tin with baking paper and then fill with dry rice, beans or baking beans. Bake for 15 minutes, remove from the oven, take out the paper and beans, brush the inside with beaten egg to seal it and bake for another 5 minutes to crisp the base. Turn the oven down by 10 degrees.

Meanwhile, make the tart filling: whisk all the ingredients together, sieve them, put them in a saucepan and heat, stirring, until warm. Pour into the tart case and bake for about 20 minutes until the lemon filling sets.

Take the tart out of the oven and allow to cool completely in the case. When cool, use a very sharp or fine serrated knife to trim the pastry – try hard not to get crumbs on the surface of the lemon tart.

Before serving sift a little icing sugar on to the surface. Light the blowtorch (this is optional) and torch it in places to caramelise the sugar – just a touch here and there. Finish by placing the lemon filaments on the surface.

BERRY TARTS

These tarts are well worth the fiddle involved in lining small tart cases. Use as many different berries as you can find: strawberries and fraises des bois, redcurrants, white currants, gooseberries, raspberries, loganberries or a mixture of any.

If you are using custard filling, prepare it in advance and allow it to cool. Heat the milk with the vanilla pod to boiling point. Remove from the heat and leave to infuse for 15 minutes. Scrape the seeds out of the vanilla pod, adding them to the warm milk.

In a bowl, mix together the egg yolks, sugar and flour to a smooth paste. Whisk in the milk until all is incorporated. Clean the pan, then pour the custard into it through a sieve. Heat the contents of the pan, stirring all the time, to boiling point. Whisk vigorously at this point, turning down the heat, for one minute to 'cook out' the flour so the custard texture is very creamy. Pour into a bowl, cover with a circle of greaseproof paper or cling film to prevent a skin forming, and allow to cool completely in the fridge. The custard will be very thick and spreadable.

Preheat the oven to 190°C/375°F/Gas mark 5. Cut 1cm/½-inch thick slices from the sweet pastry, and roll them on a floured work surface until ¼cm/¹⁄₁₀-inch thick. Pick them up with a table knife and slip into the tart cases. Press them into the tins and allow the surplus pastry to fall down the sides, to be trimmed off after baking blind. Refrigerate the tart cases for 10 minutes.

Line each tart case with a small square of baking parchment and half fill with baking beans. Bake them for 10 minutes. Take them out of the oven and remove the paper and rice. Place them back in the oven to crisp, ideally so that the top edges are lightly browned: 2–5 minutes. Remove them from the oven and allow to cool completely.

Fill each tart with cream or custard, then berries, and serve.

Makes 24 individual tarts

Equipment

Individual **tart tins** with scalloped edges – you do not need 24 as the cases can be made in batches – plus rice grains or baking beans to blind-bake

Ingredients

1 quantity **Sweet Pastry** (pages 138–139), shaped into a cylinder about 4cm wide

1.2kg/2lb 6oz **mixed berries**

For the custard filling (optional):

250ml/9fl oz **whole milk**

1 **vanilla pod**, split

4 **egg yolks**

55g/2oz **caster sugar**

25g/1oz **plain flour**

If not using custard:

Whipped double cream

REDCURRANT LAYER CAKE

Sharp redcurrants layered between thin sheets of buttery pastry make an unusual, not overly sweet yet pretty gateau that you can make up to two days in advance. Serve with crème fraîche. You can cheat and buy the pastry ready-made, but make sure it is real butter puff pastry which, thankfully, is now widely available. You can make this recipe with more or fewer layers of pastry if you wish.

Serves 8

Equipment

A baking sheet measuring 25x30cm/10x12 inches

Ingredients

1 quantity Rough Puff Pastry (pages 136–137)

Flour, for dusting

For the pastry cream:

500ml/18fl oz whole milk

1 vanilla pod or 2 teaspoons vanilla extract

6 egg yolks

100g/3 ½oz caster sugar

60g/2oz plain flour

To finish:

600g/1lb 5oz redcurrants

Icing sugar, to finish

To make the pastry cream, heat the milk with the vanilla, leave to infuse if you are using a pod and then strain. Beat the egg yolks with the sugar, sprinkle in the flour and stir until smooth. Beat in the warm milk, bit by bit, then return the whole lot to the pan. Bring to the boil, stirring constantly. The mixture will thicken. When the mixture boils, keep stirring vigorously for another minute to cook out the flour. Pour into a container and cover the surface with cling film to stop a skin forming. The pastry cream will keep for several days.

To prepare the redcurrants, wash them, then de-stalk them by holding them and running a fork down through the stalk so the berries come off – save about 3–5 stalks for decoration.

Divide the pastry into 3 pieces. Roll each piece out on a worktop dusted with flour to an approximate thickness of ¼ cm/1/10 inch, then cut each one into 2 x 20cm/8-inch squares. You should have a total of 6 squares. Place 2 on a baking sheet at once, prick all over with a fork then bake at 200°C/400°F/Gas mark 6 until golden and crisp – there must be absolutely no soggy or pale pastry or this cake will not have the right flavour and texture. Repeat twice more until there are 6 crisp squares.

Cool the pastry squares on a rack, then begin to build the gateau: place one pastry square on a flat plate and spread with a fifth of the pastry cream. Scatter over a fifth of the redcurrants. Spread another layer of pastry cream on a second square of pastry before you place it over the redcurrants, and repeat 3 more times. Leave the top pastry square bare. Just sift over a little icing sugar and decorate with redcurrants. To serve, slice with a serrated knife.

FINE APPLE TART

Likely the first tart I ever made, in an attempt to copy the Tartes Fines aux Pommes of Normandy. Admittedly I used bought puff pastry, not homemade, which works well if you want to make a quick pudding. At the bakery we find that our customers prefer it with lots of crust, so we make it in long strips and cut big slices. Most times we glaze this tart with sieved, heated apricot jam, but apple jelly, made from windfalls in autumn, is a sublime apple eating adventure.

If you want to make this a richer tart, spread custard under the apples before cooking (see page 161 for the custard recipe).

Serves 6–8

·····································

Equipment

Baking sheet measuring 25x40cm/10x15 inches

Baking parchment

·····································

Ingredients

7 or 8 eating apples

Flour, for dusting

300g/10½oz Rough Puff Pastry (pages 136–137)

To glaze:

3 tablespoons apricot jam

Juice of 1 lemon

1 tablespoon water

Or:

4 tablespoons apple jelly

Core and slice the apples into half moons about ¼cm/¹⁄₁₀-inch thick.

Preheat the oven to 220°C/425°F/Gas mark 7 and put in the baking sheet you will be using. Dust the worktop with flour and roll out the pastry to ¼cm/¹⁄₁₀-inch thickness. Pick it up, rolling it on to a well-floured rolling pin, then unroll it on to a sheet of baking parchment, placed on the baking sheet.

Use a pizza cutter or knife to cut the pastry sheet exactly in half lengthways. Arrange the apple slices in rows, one tucked under the next. We do this across the width of the pastry strips because it is easier to slice the tart later. Place 2 of the whole apple slices on each strip, evenly spaced.

Bake the tarts for 15–25 minutes until the pastry edges are golden and the apples softened – some may be appetisingly burnished by the heat. Check that the base is cooked by gently lifting a corner of the tart and looking beneath. If not quite cooked, give the tart a few more minutes, turning the oven down so you do not burn the edges. Remove from the oven and allow to cool.

While the tart cooks, put the glaze ingredients, or apple jelly if using, into a saucepan and simmer until completely dissolved. Brush the glaze gently over the whole surface of the tart, including the pastry edges, and leave for a few minutes to set. Eat at room temperature.

STRUDEL WITH SUMMER FRUITS: PEACHES, PLUMS, FIGS & GREENGAGES

Summer 'stone' fruits, poached in wine syrup, spiced lightly with cardamom and wrapped in olive oil pastry. Eat this pie with cardamom or vanilla ice cream, pouring the surplus syrup over the top. The fruit does not have to be absolutely ripe before cooking. In fact, a little bit hard is an advantage as it will not cook down to a pulp.

Serves 6–8

....

Equipment
Baking sheet measuring 25x40cm/10x15 inches, lightly greased with butter, then well dusted with flour

....

Ingredients
300ml white wine

300g caster sugar

Seeds from 4 crushed cardamom pods

4 peaches, quartered and stoned

6 red plums, halved and stoned

6 greengages, halved and stoned

6 figs, quartered

1 quantity Olive Oil Pastry (pages 140–141), made with melted butter instead of oil

Olive oil, for brushing

Icing sugar, for dusting

Preheat the oven to 190°C/375°F/Gas mark 5. Place the wine and sugar in a pan, add the cardamom seeds, place over the heat and bring to the boil. Put the peaches, plums and greengages in the syrup and cook very gently, turning occasionally, until just tender. Lift the fruit out of the syrup and put it on a plate. Set to one side with the figs.

Roll and stretch the dough as described on page 141. Once the dough measures about 40cm/15 inches across, it is ready to fill.

Trim the edges of the pastry to this size, so the thick rim of it will not be in the pie. Scatter the poached fruits over two-thirds of the pastry sheet, keeping in mind that it must fit on a 40cm baking sheet. Roll up the strudel, using floured hands. Do not worry if the odd hole or tear appears in the pastry, it will not get bigger during cooking.

Carefully pick up and put, or slide, the strudel on to the baking sheet. If the edges are untidy, they can be trimmed later. Brush the surface of the strudel with olive oil, put in the oven immediately so the pastry has no time to get soggy, and bake for 30 minutes, until it is golden.

Remove from the oven and allow to cool a little before serving. Trim the edges with a sharp or finely serrated knife. Dust the whole thing with icing sugar – not too much – and serve.

Variation
Try this pastry with mincemeat and apples for an alternative Christmas pie.

CHOCOLATE PAPER PIE WITH CHOCOLATE GANACHE & PEARS

Adding cocoa and a different type of oil to the olive oil pastry brought about this unusual, very rich chocolate pudding with pears, encased in the thinnest pastry. The filling is a type of ganache, or thick chocolate cream, but this one contains eggs and so can be baked without spoiling. Use ripe yellow pears, not green conference pears. Yellow pears have a creamy flesh that goes well with chocolate. Serve with whipped cream.

First make the pastry. Put the flour, cocoa and icing sugar into a mixing bowl, or stand mixer with dough hook attached, and mix in the oil. Add 75ml/2½fl oz of the water and mix – adding more water until you have a soft dough that does not stick to the mixing bowl but is a little tacky to touch.

Take the dough out of the mixing bowl and knead until completely smooth on a lightly floured worktop. It will feel elastic and soft. Wrap the dough in cling film and leave to rest in the fridge for half an hour.

Now make the chocolate ganache filling. Put the whipping cream in a pan with the caster sugar. Dissolve the caster sugar over a low heat, bring to the boil then remove from the heat. In a separate pan melt the chocolate over a very low temperature – it must become hotter than 40°C (just above hand-hot).

Transfer to a bowl with the cream mixture and stir the two together – the mixture will become thick. Add the melted butter and stir until glossy. Add the beaten egg yolks and mix. At this point the ganache will curdle, but beat it well with a wooden spoon for a minute or two and it will cool, come together and become quite elastic and glossy again. Cover the surface of the chocolate filling with cling film, to prevent a skin forming, and set to one side.

Take the dough from the fridge and dust the worktop with a very small amount of flour. Roll the dough into a disc, about the size of a dessert plate. Leave for 2 minutes for it to relax (making sure it is not sticking to the worktop – you may need more flour). Roll again very thin, until it is the size of a dinner plate and about ¼cm/¹⁄₁₀-inch thick.

Serves 8

....

Equipment

Baking sheet measuring 25x40cm/10x15 inches lined with baking parchment

....

Ingredients

For the pastry:

125g/4½oz Italian '00' white flour

25g/1oz cocoa powder

2 teaspoons icing sugar

1½ tablespoons groundnut or grapeseed oil

75–100ml/2½–3½fl oz iced water

For the chocolate ganache filling:

140g/5oz whipping cream

70g/2½oz caster sugar

200g/7oz unsweetened chocolate, minimum 70% cocoa solids

75g/scant 2¾oz melted butter

2 beaten egg yolks

6 ripe yellow pears, peeled, cored and cut in quarters, then placed in water with a squeeze of lemon to prevent browning

Icing sugar, for dusting

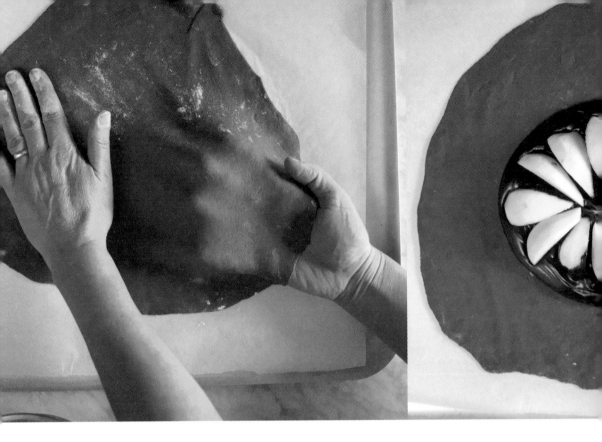

Place the disc of dough on a lightly floured baking sheet. Gently pull at the edge, holding the dough lightly in floured fingers, stretching at one point and moving around the whole circumference of the dough. The circle will expand in size until the dough roughly covers the whole of the baking sheet.

You will find that if you work patiently and slowly, and allow the dough to rest between stretching, from time to time, it will allow you to stretch it quite thin. If little tears appear, it does not matter, you will be surprised how this dough does not change shape during cooking and how the tears do not get bigger. When the dough is about 40cm/15 inches across, it is ready to fill.

Spread the chocolate filling on to the pastry base, covering an area the size of a small dinner plate. Arrange the pears in a star pattern on top of the filling then bring the surplus pastry towards the centre of the pie, gathering it in pleats at the middle. Trim off the thicker edges of the gathered pastry. Refrigerate the pie for 20 minutes.

Preheat the oven to 180°C/350°F/Gas mark 4 and bake for about 20 minutes, until the pastry has dried out and is crisp. It may leak a little in places, but do not worry as it will look tidy when removed from the baking tray after cooling. Allow to cool on the baking tray completely, then dust a little icing sugar on top. If you really want to go to town, shave a few extra bits of chocolate over the pie before dusting with icing sugar.

Cakes

When deciding which cakes to put on the counter, our philosophy at the Pocket Bakery is clear: we do not so much care that they look perfect but we believe it is all about what happens in the mouth. I'd rather a cake had a sunken appearance yet have a sublime, melting crumb than it win prizes for presentation. If there is jam in the cake, we want it to ooze out disobediently, the icing to lazily drip down the side and the centre of a chocolate cake to be juicy and medium rare, so to speak.

Beauty must be more than skin deep. Perhaps that is why we leave highly decorated cupcakes to others. My children enjoy them – yet I know it is the décor they really love to devour. Ask them what they thought of the actual cake under the fondant and they have trouble even remembering it was there at all.

I have been collecting recipes for soggy cakes since a happy year running a café in a cookbook shop, a few years before my children were born. I found a chocolate cake recipe then to which I am still devoted, and an orange cake. And I saw the advantages of substituting plain white flour, which can have a dehydrating effect on cake crumb, with ground almonds and other grains.

Such cakes never reach structural giddy heights, but it is true that we would be disappointed if they did. Succulence is what we look for. Sogginess is the grail. That is not forgetting flavour. The great taste of a cake depends to an extent on concept, or idea, but most of all it is about ingredients. I come from a generation who simply did not believe you could make a decent cake without margarine, yet now I feel a cake is not a cake without that most natural of fats and unsurpassed transporter of taste: butter.

Before we bake cakes I caution the children that we are in a rigid area of cookery. It is partly to do with cost. If you make a mistake in bread-making, the likelihood is that you will be throwing away just flour and negligible quantities of yeast and salt. With cakes it is a little more critical. Miss an item in the ingredients list or a cue in the method and there can be an expensive disaster.

The best advice for cooks is to be well organised and methodical when baking cakes. Once you have made the same type a few times you will be able to do it in future while juggling – but it is worth accepting that cake-making is a discipline first. Once you are confident, however, your instinct and creativity can come into play. Let the seasons dictate and your experience inform where you can make a clever substitution here, add an interesting ingredient there. After this, there will, we hope, only be lusciousness.

MORE ABOUT CAKE BAKING

Electric muscle. An electric mixer, either a stand mixer or hand-held electric whisk, is necessary for speed. You could safely say that a baker without one of these gadgets is like a traveller relying on horsepower long after the invention of the train. Even the cheapest hand-held electric mixers save time and stamina. Many cakes need to be 'creamed' for a long period and egg whites need to be whisked to a stiff foam to attain the right texture.

Creaming. The creaming of the butter and sugar in a cake is a very important part of the process. It creates air in the cake, visible as the mixture becomes paler in colour. During cooking this air will expand more, usually due to the addition of baking powder, to make a lighter cake.

Curdling. Do not worry if cake mixture curdles at the point where you add the eggs to the creamed butter. It will not mean a failed cake, but a slightly less light crumb. To avoid it, imagine you are making mayonnaise in reverse, and add beaten egg slowly to the cake mixture while beating.

Moulds. Try to follow the size of cake tin or mould given in the recipe as you will be able to rely on the given timings. A small selection of sizes should do: round tins measuring 18cm/7 inch, 20cm/8 inch, 23cm/9 inch and 26cm/10 inch, and 1 loaf tin 20x10x6cm/8x4x2 ½ inch. The best material for baking is simple tin or aluminium. Other types of metal can hold too much heat and have a tendency to burn the edges of cakes.

Preparing tins. Always grease tins with butter then dust the interior with flour. Greasing just the tin will not support the cake as it rises. Baking parchment, which is treated with non-stick silicone (do not confuse with greaseproof paper), is essential for lining the base of the tin. Cakes will stick even to properly buttered and floured bases. Cut circles of baking parchment, slightly larger than the base; butter the base of the tin and place the paper circle inside, then butter again, including the sides. Finally dust with flour, tapping the tin while upside down to remove excess. For wheat-free cakes, use brown rice flour.

Get organised. Gather your ingredients together before you start. Cakes often need several and it is easier than you might think to forget something vital.

Room temperature. For the best results, make sure that all the ingredients are the same temperature. Obviously butter has to be soft before being creamed but, if you keep eggs in the fridge, remember also to take them out in advance so they can reach room temperature.

Measuring. Electronic scales have revolutionised cake-making. You can weigh the ingredients into the mixing bowl as you go. When you see 'spoon' measurements, use proper measuring spoons rather than the spoons in your cutlery drawer, which are not accurate.

Folding. When a final ingredient must be incorporated into a light and airy cake mixture, and you do not want to disturb the bubbles in the mixture more than necessary, use a circular motion with a tool that 'cuts' the mixture. Traditionally bakers use a palette knife but I have learned to use a very large balloon whisk, dipping it through the mixture, and getting a better result (i.e. an airier cake). The large whisk on a stand mixer works well, held in the hand.

Cakes will not wait. Choose and prepare tins before you start making up the cake batter. An airy batter may lose its volume while you hunt for the right tin to cook it in or line a tin with baking parchment.

Oven temperatures. The temperatures given in this book are for conventional electric and not fan-assisted ovens. If you use a fan oven, reduce the temperature of the oven by 10–20°C. Always test the cake 5 minutes before it is due to be done, unless you are confident of your oven's temperature.

Unmoulding. The usual rule goes that light and airy cakes must be unmoulded from the tin immediately, and heavy or large cakes left to cool in the tin for half an hour. Heavy or large cakes tend to be more liable to cracking if unmoulded when hot.

Testing. A sponge cake made with wheat flour is done when it feels springy when pressed with a finger but the best test is to insert a skewer. If it comes out clean, the cake is done. For wheat-free cakes (there are a number in this chapter), the finger press test is enough. Also, remove a cake before it starts shrinking too much away from the sides of the tin: a sign that it is drying out.

Storing. To keep newly made cakes as fresh as possible, put them in a large plastic container with a tight-fitting lid. All sponges freeze well but make sure they are wrapped in cling film to prevent 'freezer' burn, which can dry them out.

VICTORIA MULTI-STOREY SANDWICH

It is very hard to improve on the classic sponge sandwich filled with jam, except perhaps by splitting both sponges so there are three layers of jam instead of just one. Creaming the butter and sugar for a long time until it is very light, pale and creamy ensures the sponge is light. Also, using unsalted lactic butter, such as Lurpak or French, seems to get better results. The mixture may curdle when the eggs are added but you can help prevent this if all the ingredients are the same temperature, if the butter and sugar has been creamed until almost white, and if you beat the eggs in one at a time. Note that this is the classic 'Constance Spry' method, so you weigh the eggs then use the equivalent weight for the other ingredients.

Serves 8–10

Equipment
2 x 20cm/8-inch shallow sandwich tins: generously butter, dust with flour, then line the base with baking parchment

Ingredients
6 eggs, weighed in their shells, then the same weight of:

softened butter

white caster sugar

self-raising flour or plain flour with 2 teaspoons baking powder

450g/1lb raspberry, strawberry or plum jam or a different jam for each layer

Caster sugar, for dusting

For the white chocolate glaze:

100g/3½oz double cream

15g/1½oz softened butter

85g/3oz white chocolate, chopped

Preheat the oven to 180°C/350°F/Gas mark 4 and prepare the tins. Put the butter into the bowl of a stand mixer and beat until pale. Add the sugar and beat again for several minutes until the mixture is almost white, occassionally scraping down the sides with a spatula. Add the eggs, cracking them into a small dish and adding one by one, beating well between each egg then continuing to beat for another 3 minutes afterwards – the mixture will seem almost gelatinous. If you do this and the previous stage thoroughly, the mixture will not curdle. If it does, add a dessertspoon of the flour but the sponge will not be quite as light.

Finally, very slowly fold in the flour using a palette knife, or large table knife, lifting the batter and working in a figure-of-eight pattern so the flour is gradually incorporated. Spoon the cake batter evenly into the tins, spreading them very lightly with a knife. Bake for 25–35 minutes until the surface feels springy. Insert a skewer into the cake and if it comes out clean the cake is done. Run a knife around the edge of the cakes and immediately turn out on to a rack to cool.

When the cakes are cool, cut both in half horizontally, then sandwich them together with the jam. To make the glaze, heat the cream to just before boiling point then remove from the heat. Put the butter and chocolate into a bowl and add the hot cream. Leave for a minute, then stir to make a smooth glaze. Allow to cool slightly before pouring over the cake and allowing it to drip down the sides.

CITRUS SYRUP CAKE

An interesting gateau made with goat's butter that has a blissful, fine crumb and goes well with the sharpness of lemon. Suitable for people intolerant to dairy (defined as cow's milk).

Serves 8

....

Equipment

25cm/10-inch square cake with loose base: butter the tin, line the base with baking parchment, butter again then dust with flour

....

Ingredients

115g/4oz softened goat's butter

225g/8oz caster sugar

4 eggs, separated, the yolks beaten

175g/6oz self-raising flour, sifted

55g/2oz plain flour

½ teaspoon baking powder

Grated zest and juice of 2 (unwaxed or scrubbed) lemons

For the syrup:

150g/5½oz granulated sugar

Juice of 2 lemons (4 tablespoons)

For the filling:

55g/2oz fresh goat's curd cheese

30g/1oz caster sugar

Zest of 1 lemon

2 tablespoons nibbed sugar, to decorate

Preheat the oven to 180°C/350°F/Gas mark 4 and prepare the tin. Cream the butter and sugar, whisking until very white and fluffy (an electric whisk is recommended). Whisk in the egg yolks, scraping down the sides of the bowl with a spatula. Sift in the flours with the baking powder, then fold into the cake batter with the lemon zest and juice, using a metal spoon.

Whisk the egg whites in a separate bowl until you have stiff white foam; stir one tablespoon into the mixture then fold in the rest, carefully so as not to break down the foam too much. Transfer to the prepared cake tin, and level the top with a spatula.

Put the cake in the oven – you will notice, as I did when I had a peep, that it will collapse into slightly lumpy batter before rising again. Bake for about 30 minutes until pale gold and firm to the touch. To test for doneness, insert a skewer into the cake and pull it out. The cake is done if the skewer comes out clean.

Remove from the oven and turn out carefully on to a rack. Allow to become completely cool, then slice into two halves, horizontally.

To make the syrup: soak the sugar in the lemon juice then boil together until you have a light syrup. Drizzle this over the two halves of cake.

Make the filling, combining the goat's curd cheese with the sugar and most of the lemon zest, then spreading it over one half of the cake. Sandwich the two together then sprinkle the nibbed sugar and remaining lemon zest over the top.

WINTER RHUBARB UPSIDE-DOWN CAKE

This cake makes use of winter rhubarb, the bright pink rhubarb forced to grow indoors. It is more fragrant than summer green rhubarb, and baked with sugar under a sponge becomes lightly caramelised. Avoid using a loose-based tin with this cake as it tends to leak. Serve with custard or cream.

Preheat the oven to 175°C/325°F/Gas mark 3 and prepare the dish. Lay the rhubarb pieces side by side on a baking tray and bake for 15 minutes to soften and dry out a little. Allow to cool.

Scatter the Demerara sugar all over the base of the buttered dish, then follow with the rhubarb pieces, being careful to keep them whole.

Put the ground almonds, flour, baking powder and milk into the stand mixer bowl and whisk together by hand to distribute. Add the sugar, butter and eggs and beat in the mixer all together until pale and increased in volume. Spread the mixture over the rhubarb, trying not to disturb it too much. Smooth the surface with a spatula.

Bake for about 35–40 minutes until the cake is golden. To test for doneness, insert a skewer into the cake and pull it out. The cake is done if the skewer comes out clean. Allow to cool in the dish for 5 minutes.

Meanwhile, make the syrup. Boil the rhubarb, water and sugar together until syrupy, then pass through a sieve. Invert a shallow flat-based serving dish on top of the cake. Swiftly up-end it so the hot juices do not spill everywhere – especially on you – and turn out the cake. Pour the syrup over the cake and serve it warm.

Serves 8

Equipment

30cm oval ovenproof dish with straight sides, preferably made from enamelled tin/iron (such as Le Creuset), buttered with 30g/1oz butter

Ingredients

450g/1lb pink winter rhubarb, cut into 5cm/2-inch sticks

50g/1¾oz Demerara sugar

100g/3½oz ground almonds

100g/3½oz sifted self-raising flour

2 teaspoons baking powder

2 tablespoons milk

250g/9oz golden caster sugar

250g/9oz softened butter

4 eggs

For the syrup:

100g extra rhubarb, chopped

3 tablespoons water

100g/3½oz sugar

COCOA CAKE

A wonderful chocolate cake, made with no flour at all and, unusually, no melted chocolate but cocoa. I think it is a superior cake to other chocolate cakes because it has all the flavour and goodness of chocolate, but butter in place of the fat in a chocolate bar. This cake makes a good pudding, served with crème fraîche, which suits its own non-rich texture.

Preheat the oven to 180°C/350°F/Gas mark 4 and prepare the tin. Put the cocoa in a small bowl and add the hot water and vanilla. Mix with a small whisk – you will find if you leave it a few minutes all the lumps will whisk out.

Put the butter into the bowl of a stand mixer and beat until pale. Add all but 50g/1¾oz of the sugar and beat again until the mixture is almost white. From time to time, scrape down the sides with a spatula. This may take several minutes, and the sugar will mostly dissolve in the process.

Beat in the egg yolks, followed by the (cooled) cocoa mixture and almonds. Continue to beat – the mixture will turn slightly paler as it is aerated.

Put the egg whites into a separate bowl and whisk with the salt until foamy. Add the cream of tartar (to set the foam) and then whisk until soft white peaks of foam are formed. Add the remaining sugar then whisk until the peaks of foam are firm. Stir one large heaped tablespoon of the egg white into the cake mixture to loosen it, then fold in the rest with a large balloon whisk (the whisk on the stand mixer is ideal) or a knife. By dipping the whisk slowly through the mixture, you will not disturb the air in it too much.

Spoon or pour the cake into the tin, and spread it out to the edges gently using a knife. Bake the cake for 60–70 minutes. It will rise up but it will fall again – even sink a little. We like this because it is a sign of a luscious cake. Remove the cake from the tin but allow it to cool on the base – it is very fragile.

To make the glaze, put the chocolate into a bowl. Put the double cream in a pan and heat to boiling point. Pour over the chocolate and leave for 2 minutes. Stir until you have a dark glossy cream, then pour over the cake and spread to the edges. It is nice if a little of the glaze drips down the sides.

Serves 8–10

. . . .

Equipment

25cm/10-inch cake tin with loose base: butter the tin, line the base with baking parchment, butter again then dust with flour

. . . .

Ingredients

50g/1¾oz cocoa

100g/3½oz boiling water

1 teaspoon vanilla extract

225g/8oz softened butter

225g/8oz caster sugar

6 eggs, separated

170g/6oz ground almonds, toasted

Pinch salt

¾ teaspoon cream of tartar

For the glaze:

100g/3½oz unsweetened chocolate, broken into pieces

100ml/3½fl oz double cream

CHILDREN'S CHOCOLATE CAKE

This is another sandwich cake, this time made with flour and very typical of the kind my children like in that it contains lots of buttercream and lashings of icing. The recipe is adapted from the Classic Tearoom Chocolate Victoria Cake in Annie Bell's excellent Baking Bible. You can mix all the cake ingredients at once, making this a very swift cake to bake.

Serves 8–10

Equipment

2 x 18cm/7-inch cake tins:
butter the tins, line the base with
baking parchment, butter again
then dust with flour

Ingredients

225g/8oz butter, diced

225g/8oz golden caster sugar

175g/6oz self-raising flour, sifted

50g/1¾oz cocoa powder, sifted

2 teaspoons baking
powder, sifted

¼ teaspoon fine sea salt

1 teaspoon vanilla extract

4 eggs

100ml/3½fl oz milk

For the buttercream:

100g/3½oz softened butter

100g/3½oz icing sugar, sifted

2 teaspoons cocoa, sifted

1 egg yolk

For the icing:

100g/3½oz milk chocolate,
broken into pieces

15g/½oz butter

30g/1oz cocoa powder

50ml/2fl oz coffee, or water

1 tablespoon golden syrup

Preheat the oven to 170°C/325°F/Gas mark 3 and prepare the tins. Place all the cake ingredients in a food processor or a stand mixer and cream together – you will need to scrape the sides down from time to time. Transfer to the cake tins, smooth the surface with a knife and bake for 35–45 minutes until a skewer inserted in the centre comes out clean. Run a knife around the edge and leave to cool completely.

To make the buttercream, blend the butter, icing sugar and cocoa together in a medium-sized bowl then whisk with an electric whisk on high speed for 2 minutes until very pale and fluffy. Add the egg yolk and whisk for a minute longer.

Remove the cakes from the tin and put one on a stand or plate. Spread the bottom half with the buttercream, then sandwich with the top half.

To make the icing, put all the icing ingredients in a pan and whisk together over a very low heat. Be careful not to burn the contents. Leave to cool a little, and thicken, then smooth all over the top of the cake and leave the icing to drip down the sides.

ORANGE CAKE

A butter cake with a fine, soft crumb, baked in a loaf tin and iced with buttercream. Make it in a loaf tin, an ideal shape to cut slices from for packed lunches.

Serves 6

Equipment

20x10cm/8x4-inch loaf tin: butter the tin, line the base with baking parchment, butter again then dust with flour

Ingredients

100g/3½oz self-raising flour

50g/1¾oz plain white flour

150g/5½ oz caster sugar

Zest of 2 oranges – about 1 tablespoon

Pinch salt

3 eggs

3 tablespoons milk

150g/5½oz softened butter

For the buttercream:

100g caster sugar

60ml/4 tablespoons orange juice

3 egg yolks

225g/8oz butter

Zest of 2 oranges – about 1 tablespoon

Orange jelly diamonds (optional decoration)

Preheat the oven to 180°C/350°F/Gas mark 4 and prepare the tin. Whisk together the two flours in a large bowl or stand mixer and add the caster sugar, orange zest and salt. In a separate bowl, beat together the eggs and milk. Add the butter to the flours with about half the milk and egg mixture and beat slowly to roughly incorporate. Turn up the speed and beat until the mixture becomes lighter coloured and a little bulkier. Scrape the sides of the bowl with a spatula from time to time.

Beat in the remaining milk and egg mixture, bit by bit. Scrape down the sides once all is added, then beat for one minute. Transfer the cake mixture to the tin, smooth the top with a knife; bake for 1 hour (covering the tin with a sheet of aluminium foil to prevent over-browning). Check to see if the cake is done: insert a skewer into the cake. The cake is done if the skewer comes out clean. Cool for a few minutes in the tin, running a knife down the sides as soon as it comes out of the oven. Turn out on to a rack; cool completely then wrap in foil for an hour or two.

To make the buttercream, boil the sugar and orange juice together in a small pan until thickened and syrupy. Transfer to a small heatproof jug. Beat the egg yolks in a separate bowl with a hand mixer; add the syrup slowly. Continue to beat for a minute or two then allow to become completely cool. Finally beat in the butter with the orange zest. Spread all over the top of the cake, and allow to set. Decorate, if you like, with orange jelly diamonds.

BOILED CAKES

A convenient method that does away with creaming butter and sugar, which is especially suitable for loaf cakes made with fresh fruit, dried fruit and even vegetables. You begin by boiling together the butter, sugar and either golden syrup, black treacle or other fruit syrup. The mixture must be cooled a little before the eggs are added, and finally the dry ingredients. These cakes have a wonderful, sticky toffee edge and do not contain wheat flour. The mixture will seem very wet when you first put it in the tin and will not appear to be cooking at all in the first half hour in the oven. It will, however, suddenly turn pale brown within the last 15–20 minutes. These cakes are always cooked on a low temperature, 150°C/300°F/Gas mark 2, otherwise they will burn.

FUDGY BANANA CAKE

Gorgeously sticky at the sides and soggy in the middle, this cake tastes better made with slightly unripe bananas, i.e. those with no black spots.

Serves 8

Equipment

20x10cm/8x4-inch loaf tin;
butter the tin, line the base with
baking parchment, butter again
then dust with flour

Ingredients

125g/4½oz agave syrup

125g/4½oz Demerara sugar

125g/4½oz butter

¼ teaspoon allspice

1 teaspoon ground cinnamon

2 eggs, beaten with 1 pinch salt

3 small bananas, lightly mashed

250g/9oz ground almonds

To glaze (optional):

3 tablespoons apricot jam

1 tablespoon water

Squeeze of lemon juice

Preheat the oven to 150°C/300°F/Gas mark 2 and prepare the tin. Put the syrup, sugar and butter in a pan. Allow the butter to melt, bring to the boil and boil – not too hard – for 3 minutes. Remove from the heat and allow to cool for about 10 minutes. Add the spices and beat in the eggs. Stir in the banana then the ground almonds. Scrape into the prepared tin, and bake for about 1 hour 10 minutes or until golden and a little puffed. When done, the cake will feel springy to the touch.

Remove from the oven and cool in the tin. This cake is very fragile when hot so allow it to cool for about 10 minutes before removing it from the tin.

Boil the ingredients for the glaze together, if using, then pass through a sieve. Paint all over the cake.

GINGER SYRUP CAKE

A favourite cake my family have been making in one form or another for many years. My mother made this cake to Constance Spry's Belvoir Cake recipe, laboriously creaming the butter and sugar. I tried the boiling method one day when I had forgotten to take the butter out of the fridge, and think it gives the cake a toffee stickiness it had lacked before. This cake improves and becomes yet more intensely gingery four days after being made, and will keep for several weeks in a tin.

Preheat the oven to 150°C/300°F/Gas mark 2 and prepare the tin. Put the treacle, sugar and butter in a pan. Allow the butter to melt, bring to the boil and boil – not too hard – for 3 minutes. Remove from the heat and allow to cool for about 10 minutes. Add the ground ginger and beat in the eggs. Stir in half the crystallised ginger, followed by the ground almonds. Put the flour and bicarbonate of soda in a separate bowl and whisk together for a few seconds. Fold into the cake mixture. Transfer to the prepared tin and bake for 1 hour–1 hour 15 minutes. To test if it is done, insert a skewer into the cake. The cake is done if the skewer comes out clean. Allow to cool in the tin.

Boil the ingredients for the glaze together then pass through a sieve. Paint all over the cake. Scatter over the remaining crystallised ginger.

Serves 12

. . . .

Equipment

20cm/10-inch square cake tin with loose base: butter the tin, line the base with baking parchment, butter again then dust with flour

. . . .

Ingredients

200g/7oz black treacle

200g/7oz muscovado sugar

200g/7oz butter

2 teaspoons ground ginger

3 eggs, beaten

150g/4oz crystallised ginger, sliced

200g/7oz ground almonds

175g/6oz plain flour

1 teaspoon bicarbonate of soda

To glaze:

3 tablespoons apricot jam

1 tablespoon water

Squeeze of lemon juice

TOFFEE APPLE PUMPKIN CAKE

We made this cake for Halloween the first year the Pocket Bakery opened at the Doodle Bar. The bar was unforgettably, brilliantly decorated with a giant paper skeleton, and the cake – an experiment on the day – a huge success. We carried on making it through the winter, and now make it throughout the rest of the year, using butternut squash if pumpkin is not available.

Preheat the oven to 150°C/300°F/Gas mark 2 and prepare the tin. Peel and core the apple and put it, with the pumpkin flesh, in a food processor and chop very small. Put the syrup, sugar and butter in a pan. Allow the butter to melt, bring to the boil and boil – not too hard – for 3 minutes. Remove from the heat and allow to cool for about 10 minutes. Add the nutmeg and beat in the eggs. Stir in the apple and pumpkin, followed by the ground almonds. Bake for 1 hour and 15 minutes – 1½ hours. To test for doneness, insert a skewer into the cake and pull it out. The cake is done if the skewer comes out clean. Cool in the tin.

Boil the ingredients for the glaze together then pass through a sieve. Paint all over the cake. Decorate with pumpkin slices.

Serves 8

Equipment

20x10cm/8x4-inch loaf tin; butter the tin, line the base with baking parchment, butter again then dust with flour

Ingredients

1 dessert apple

150g/5½oz pumpkin flesh

125g/4½oz golden syrup

125g/4½oz Demerara sugar

125g/4½oz butter

½ teaspoon grated nutmeg

2 eggs, beaten

250g/9oz ground almonds

To glaze and decorate:

3 tablespoons apricot jam

1 tablespoon water

Squeeze of lemon juice

Thin slices of raw pumpkin, cut into Halloween pumpkin shapes

PLUM CAKE

Another soggy fruit cake, which, if it does not fall into soft,
fruity clods on the plate after slicing, is not the job. This cake
is just as good a lunchbox cake as a grown-up fruit cake to
decorate with gold and candied fruits for Christmas.

Serves 8

· ·

Equipment

18cm/7-inch round cake tin
(10cm/4-inch deep) with loose
base: butter the tin, line the base
with baking parchment, butter
again then dust with flour.
To insulate for a longer cooking
time, wrap 3 layers of baking
parchment around the tin and
secure with string.

· ·

Ingredients

125g/4½oz golden syrup

125g/4½oz soft dark brown sugar

125g/4½oz butter

85g/3oz pitted prunes, halved

85g/3oz raisins

85g/3oz sultanas

1 teaspoon mixed spice

1 teaspoon cinnamon

2 eggs, beaten

1 small dessert apple, grated

250g ground almonds

To glaze and decorate:

3 tablespoons apricot jam

1 tablespoon water

Squeeze of lemon juice

Candied orange, kumquats
or other fruit, edible gold leaf
(optional decoration)

Preheat the oven to 150°C/300°F/Gas mark 2 and prepare the tin. Put the syrup, sugar, butter and dried fruit in a pan. Allow the butter to melt, bring to the boil and boil – not too hard – for 3 minutes. Remove from the heat and allow to cool for about 10 minutes. Add the spices and beat in the eggs. Stir in the grated apple and ground almonds and transfer to the cake tin.

Bake for 1 hour and 45 minutes to 2 hours. The cake will rise a little but not much. To test for doneness, insert a skewer into the cake and pull it out. The cake is done if the skewer comes out clean. Allow to cool in the tin.

Boil the jam, water and lemon juice together then pass through a sieve. Paint all over the cake. Decorate with candied orange and a little gold leaf, if desired.

PRALINE CAKE WITH RASPBERRY & ROSE MESS

A succulent cake to serve for pudding or tea, the flavour is made more intensely nutty by adding melted, caramelised butter. The mixture contains only egg yolks; freeze the whites to use in the fruit meringue cake. The inner cream contains hazelnut paste, which can be bought online (see Suppliers, page 246).

Preheat the oven to 180°C/350°F/Gas mark 4 and prepare the tin. Put the butter in a pan and heat until it has melted and simmers gently. Let the butter boil until the solids in the bottom of the pan turn a golden brown and the butter smells fragrantly nutty. Pour it through a sieve into a glass jug to prevent further cooking, and set to one side.

Toast the hazelnuts over a medium heat in a dry pan, then grind to a powder in a food processor. Put in a bowl with the cornflour and whisk the two together. Set to one side.

Put the egg yolks and sugar in a food processor and whisk until pale and nearly triple the volume. This may take several minutes. Whisk in the water then stop the mixer, remove the bowl with the cake mixture in it and add half the hazelnut mixture. Fold in by gently dipping and lifting the large whisk, or a balloon whisk, through the cake mixture.

Fold the remaining hazelnut mixture in the same manner. Finally add the sieved brown butter, dropping it in slowly from a height of 25cm/10 inches to cool it as it falls into the mixture. Fold in and then scrape the cake mixture into the tin.

Smooth the surface with a knife and bake for 35–40 minutes until the cake is firm when pressed. To test for doneness, insert a skewer into the cake and pull it out. The cake is done if the skewer comes out clean.

Remove the cake from the oven and cool in the tin. Unmould and place on a rack then cut it in half horizontally. Separate the two halves – carefully, because the cake is very fragile – and drizzle over the hazelnut liqueur, if using. Combine the filling ingredients, spread on one half of the cake and sandwich the two together.

For the decoration, combine the whipped cream with the icing sugar and spread it smoothly on the sides of the cake. Press the chopped hazelnuts on to the sides (if you are very confident handling the cake, put the chopped hazelnuts on a plate; pick up the cake and hold firmly between two hands then roll the creamed edges in the nuts).

To finish, simply dust the surface with icing sugar. For more décor, arrange a little pile of raspberries and fresh red rose petals in the centre.

Serves 6

Equipment

23cm/9-inch cake tin with loose base: butter the tin, line the base with baking parchment, butter again then dust with flour

Ingredients

85g/3oz butter

115g/4oz skinned hazelnuts

30g/1oz cornflour

12 egg yolks

175g/6oz caster sugar

60ml/4 tablespoons water

4 tablespoons Frangelico (hazelnut liqueur), optional

For the filling:

200g/7oz raspberries

60g/2oz hazelnut paste or same quantity ground hazelnuts

150ml/¼ pint double cream, whipped

1 teaspoon rose water

2 tablespoons sifted icing sugar

For the decoration:

150ml/¼ pint double cream, whipped until firm

1 tablespoon sifted icing sugar

150g/3½oz skinned hazelnuts, toasted in a dry pan and finely chopped

Extra icing sugar for dusting

Raspberries and edible deep red rose petals (optional decoration)

PASSION FRUIT MERINGUE CAKE WITH GREEN TEA CREAM

Against the high sweetness of meringue, the intriguing flavour of bitter green tea and exotic passion fruit flesh triumph in a romantically pretty cake. The meringue should be soft in the centre but some like theirs a little more crisp and caramelised. Bake for an extra 20 minutes if so.

Preheat the oven to 100°C/200°F/less than Gas mark ¼, and prepare the tin. Put the egg whites in a mixing bowl/stand mixer and whisk until soft peaks of white foam form. Gradually sprinkle in the caster sugar, as you whisk, and then continue to whisk for a few minutes until the egg whites are firm and stiff.

Add the sifted icing sugar and continue to whisk – the mixture should eventually become very shiny and stiff. Scoop the mixture into the piping bag and pipe a heart shape on to each of the baking sheets. Bake for 1 hour and 45 minutes, then turn off the oven and leave the door open. When cool, remove the meringues from the oven.

While the meringues become completely cold, combine the green tea, sugar and cream. Spread on the surface of one meringue, then scoop small amounts of the passion fruit in evenly spaced little blobs, on to the cream. Place the second meringue on top and then decorate with rose petals or mint leaves.

Serves 4

Equipment

2 baking sheets lined with baking parchment

Piping bag – or use a plastic bag with a hole snipped off the corner as a makeshift piping bag

Ingredients

3 egg whites

90g/3¼oz caster sugar

90g/3¼oz sifted icing sugar

For the cream:

2 teaspoons green tea powder

2 tablespoons sugar

225ml/8fl oz double cream, whipped

2 passion fruit, split in half

Edible rose petals or fresh mint leaves, to decorate (optional)

TIRAMISU ROULADE

Not straying too far from the pleasures of tiramisu, a luscious, fragile roulade made from the lightest vanilla sponge, soaked with coffee, filled with mascarpone and dusted with cocoa.

Serves 8

. . . .

Equipment

20x30cm/8x12 inch Swiss roll tin: butter the tin, line the base with baking parchment then butter again and dust with flour

. . . .

Ingredients

For the roulade:

35g/1¼oz plain flour

25g/1oz cornflour

4 eggs, separated

2 whole eggs

115g/4oz caster sugar

5g/⅛oz vanilla extract

¼ teaspoon cream of tartar

75ml/5 tablespoons Marsala (optional)

150ml/5fl oz fresh coffee, strong but not espresso strength

For the filling:

3 eggs, separated

125g/4oz caster sugar

225g/8oz mascarpone

Cocoa powder, for dusting

Preheat the oven to 180°C/350°F/Gas mark 4 and prepare the tin. To make the cake: sift the flour into a bowl, add the cornflour and whisk the two together. Use a stand mixer or hand whisk to whisk the egg yolks, whole eggs and all but 2 teaspoons of the sugar until pale cream-coloured and at least doubled in volume.

Add the vanilla, then sift half the flour mixture on to the surface and use a hand-held balloon whisk to gently, by dipping and lifting the mixture, fold it in. Sift in the remaining flour, and repeat the folding until all the flour is incorporated.

Whisk the egg whites for the cake, adding the cream of tartar. Once the eggs form soft white peaks, add the reserved 2 teaspoons of sugar and continue to whisk until the peaks are firm and glossy. Fold the egg whites into the cake batter (again with a balloon whisk) and then immediately transfer to the tin. Level the mixture by sweeping a palette knife across the tin.

Bake for 7–10 minutes until the surface of the cake is an even pale brown – do not worry if it does not feel springy to touch, it is meant to be a little collapsible (don't bother with the skewer test either). Remove from the oven, cover with a cloth and then invert on to the table. Remove the tin, and roll up the roulade in the cloth. Leave it rolled as it cools.

Meanwhile make the filling. Put the egg yolks and sugar in a bowl and whisk until pale, then fold in the mascarpone. Whisk the egg whites in a separate bowl and then fold into the mascarpone mixture.

To assemble: combine the Marsala (if using) and coffee. Unroll the roulade and remove the cloth. Drip the coffee mixture all over the inside surface until it becomes quite soggy. Spread the mascarpone mixture all over the surface, sift cocoa powder over the mascarpone mixture, and roll up the roulade. Refrigerate for at least 1 hour before serving.

ORANGE POLENTA CAKE

A 'young' type of cake that has become a classic – testament to a growing interest in alternative grains and their use in baking. We like to alternate the type of citrus fruit used in it, depending on the season. In December we make it with bergamot, a sour orange of sorts; in January it can be made with the first new season, extra sweet primofiore lemons, or Seville oranges; in February try it with blood oranges. Serve with Greek yoghurt as a delicious pudding. It is better to use natural, coarse ground polenta than the instant type.

Preheat the oven to 170°C/325°F/Gas mark 3 and prepare the tin. Beat the butter, sugar and vanilla together until light and creamy. The Demerara sugar will not dissolve until it is cooked, so don't worry if it appears gritty. Beat in the eggs one by one and finally stir in the ground almonds, polenta, orange zest and baking powder. The batter will appear thick and heavy.

Pour into the tin and bake for 40–50 minutes until the surface is light brown and the cake is coming slightly away from the sides. Remove from the oven, cool for 10 minutes then turn out. This cake will only just set, rather than dry out like other sponges. Handle it carefully as you remove from the tin as it is quite fragile.

To make the syrup, boil the orange juice and sugar together until slightly reduced. Allow to cool then prick the cake all over with a skewer before brushing the syrup over the surface and sides.

To decorate, if desired, scatter over the pistachios and the pomegranate seeds, plus the orange zest. Mix the icing sugar with the orange juice and put it in a freezer bag or strong plastic bag. Snip off the corner and use as an improvised piping bag to pipe zigzag patterns all over the surface of the cake.

Serves 6–8

. . . .

Equipment

20–25cm/8–10-inch springform tin: butter the tin, line with baking parchment, then butter once more

. . . .

Ingredients

200g/7oz softened butter

200g/7oz Demerara sugar

1 teaspoon vanilla extract

3 eggs

200g/7oz ground almonds

100g/3½oz coarse polenta meal

Zest of 2 oranges

1 teaspoon baking powder

For the syrup:

Juice of 2 oranges

120g caster sugar

For the decoration (optional):

2 tablespoons chopped unsalted shelled pistachios

Pomegranate seeds

Grated orange zest

100g/3½oz icing sugar

2½ teaspoons orange juice, strained

RASPBERRY RING

A light, sweet but buttery sponge with fresh berries buried inside, and a little pot of raspberry jam to eat with it. This is a great cake to make if you do not have an electric mixer. The ring mould is optional – you could use an ordinary cake mould – but I like to put a small pot of jam in the centre of the mould to serve it.

Serves 6
....

Equipment

22cm/8-inch ring mould cake tin (savarin mould) or 18cm/7-inch round cake tin: butter the tin well, then dust with flour
....

Ingredients

60g/2¼oz plain flour

½ teaspoon baking powder

180g/6¼oz icing sugar

70g/2½oz ground almonds

6 egg whites

100g/3½oz butter

200g/7oz raspberries

To serve:

Icing sugar

125g/4½oz raspberry jam

Clotted cream (optional)

Preheat the oven to 180°C/350°F/Gas mark 4 and prepare the tin. Sift the flour into a bowl with the baking powder, icing sugar and ground almonds and whisk them together. Beat in the egg whites. Put the butter in a pan, allow it to melt then turn up the heat a little and allow it to simmer until the solids in the base of the pan begin to turn golden brown. Immediately pour the butter into the bowl with the flour-almond mixture and mix well. Allow to cool.

Place the raspberries for the cake in the base of the ring mould. Spoon the cake batter over the top of them, letting it fall naturally around the fruit. Bake for 20 minutes – the sponge will feel springy to the touch when the cake is done.

Leave it in the tin to cool for 10 minutes then turn out on to a plate. Dust very lightly with icing sugar so it does not obliterate the sight of the raspberries peeping through the sponge. Put the raspberry jam into a small pot or shot glass and place it in the middle of the cake with a spoon in it. Eat slices of the cake with the jam and cream – like a very rich cream tea.

FRUIT PECAN MACAROON

A cake that is made like a meringue, but once made is more like a cake, being packed full of fruit and nuts. The texture is similar to a macaroon, being soggy and sticky inside. Ever since making this cake for the first time 20 years ago, I have been amazed by the flavour: a natural toffee taste that emerges when you combine the pecans – no other nut will do – with the other preserved fruits. I have served this cake as an alternative Christmas cake, to great applause.

Preheat the oven to 150°C/300°F/Gas mark 2 and prepare the baking sheets and rings. Put the egg whites and sugar in the bowl of a stand mixer and whisk to combine. Turn up the speed to full and whisk for about 10 minutes until the mixture forms stiff peaks when you draw a spoon through it.

Fold the chopped pecans and dried fruits into the meringue, making sure they are evenly distributed. Place a cake ring on each baking sheet and spoon an even amount of the mixture into them. Smooth the surface with a spatula but lift it quickly in places to create little peaks that will look crisp and delicious when the cake is finished.

Bake for 35–40 minutes, until the cakes are pale brown. They may crack in places but it does not matter. Allow both cakes to cool completely, then turn one cake carefully over and place it on a cake stand or plate. Spread the cream all over the surface, then add your chosen fruit. Cover with the second cake, lifting it on carefully so as not to crack it.

Serves 6–8

Equipment

2 x 30cm/12-inch square baking sheets, lined with baking parchment

2 x 23cm/9-inch cake rings, lightly greased with groundnut or sunflower oil

Ingredients

4 egg whites

250g/9oz golden icing sugar, sifted

90g/3oz pecan nuts, finely chopped

90g/3oz dried apricots, finely chopped

90g/3oz dates, finely chopped

For the filling:

300ml/10fl oz double cream, whipped

250g/9oz fresh fruit – exotic fruit pulp seems to match this well. For winter: lychees (shelled and stoned), pomegranate seeds, passion fruit flesh. For summer: ripe green or black figs, fresh ripe apricots, slices of ripe yellow peaches

Optional decoration:

A heap of sugared dates, stuffed with pecans (brush the dates with egg white and roll in granulated sugar). Fresh sprigs of mint or if you can find them, Provençal glacé apricots.

RICOTTA CHEESECAKE WITH ROASTED PEACHES & TOASTED PINENUTS

Just to show you what a real cheesecake is, setting aside all those industrial versions, we want to encourage you to make your own biscuit base. We like to pile the berries in the centre to give this amazing flavoured, creamy-textured cake real presence. You will need to let the ricotta drain in a sieve, placed over a bowl, in the fridge for about 2 hours to dry it out a bit. Real buffalo ricotta makes a very special cheesecake.

To make the biscuit base: cream 80g/2¾oz of the butter with the sugar in a stand mixer until pale and light textured. Add the egg, vanilla, flour, baking powder and salt. Mix to a dough then turn the dough out on to the worktop. Form into a ball, and chill the dough for 30 minutes.

Preheat the oven to 180°C/350°F/Gas mark 4. Take the dough from the fridge and roll out very thinly, to about ½cm/¼ inch. Place on a baking sheet lined with baking paper and bake for 15 minutes until dry and golden brown. Allow to cool, then either put in a food processor and process to crumbs, or put in a plastic bag, breaking the biscuit into pieces, and smash to crumbs with a rolling pin. Put the crumbs into a bowl.

Melt the remaining butter, and add to the crumbs in the bowl. Tip the crumbs into the tin, then press them into the base, nice and evenly, using your hands.

Preheat the oven to 190°C/375°F/Gas mark 5, ready to bake the cheesecake. Toast the pine nuts in a pan until golden then put them on a plate so they do not continue to cook. Put the remaining filling ingredients in the stand mixer and whisk for about 5 minutes (or use a hand-held electric whisk).

Stir in the pine nuts. Spoon the mixture into the tin, and smooth the surface with a spatula. Bake for about 1 hour. The surface will be quite brown. Leave to cool in the tin.

While the cheesecake cooks, prepare the peaches. Put the vanilla, syrup and Marsala in a heavy-based shallow pan and place over a medium heat until the mixture boils. Put the peach quarters in the pan, and cook, carefully turning them over from time to time, until they are just becoming tender.

Sprinkle over the caster sugar, and turn up the heat so the peaches brown in places where the sugar caramelises – don't stir. Allow the peaches to cool. Dust the surface of the cheesecake with icing sugar. Heap the pan-cooked peaches into the centre and scatter over the pine nuts.

Serves 6

Equipment

22cm/8-inch round cake tin with loose base, buttered

Ingredients

For the biscuit base:

120g/4½oz softened butter

165g/6oz Demerara sugar

1 egg

¼ teaspoon vanilla extract

225g/7½oz plain flour

¾ teaspoon baking powder

Pinch salt

For the filling:

125g/4oz pine nuts

1kg/2lb 4oz ricotta, drained in a sieve for 30 minutes

180ml/6fl oz double cream

4 eggs

125g/4½oz caster sugar

A few gratings of nutmeg

40g/1½oz plain flour

For the topping:

½ teaspoon vanilla extract

60g/2oz agave syrup or golden syrup

2 tablespoons Marsala, or sweet sherry

4 peaches, stoned, quartered (it helps if they are not too ripe)

1 heaped teaspoon caster sugar

To serve:

Icing sugar, for dusting

2 tablespoons pine nuts, toasted until golden in a dry pan

JAMMY ROLL CAKE

In the summer of 2012 we baked for our local Diamond Jubilee street party and created this striking cake that is a celebration of the deliciousness of English strawberry jam as much as anything else. The cakes, which sit side by side in a covering of fondant icing, are made from butter-free whipped genoise sponge – they need to be as airy as possible so follow the gentle 'whisk folding' instructions carefully. Also, do not overcook – they should be pale in colour, just set and soft so they can be rolled up without cracking.

Preheat the oven to 230°C/450°F/Gas mark 8 and prepare the tins. Whisk together the flour and cornflour in a small bowl so they are well mixed and set aside. Separate 2 of the eggs, putting the whites in a bowl ready to whisk later. Put the yolks, the other two eggs and the egg yolk in a mixing bowl with 100g/3½oz of the sugar.

Whisk at high speed for about 3 minutes until the mixture is pale yellow and three times the volume. Add the vanilla and whisk again briefly. The next stage must be done carefully. Add half the flour, then using a large balloon whisk (I use the one from my electric mixer), fold in the flour by gently dipping the whisk through the egg mixture a few times. It will become slightly firmer and more stable. Very carefully, using the same technique, fold in the remaining flour, being careful to retain the air in the cake mixture as much as possible.

In a separate bowl, whisk the egg whites with the cream of tartar until stiff; add the remaining 15g/½oz caster sugar and whisk again until glossy and firm. Using the same whisk 'dipping' technique, fold the egg whites into the cake mixture, until they are evenly incorporated. Try not to lose any of the volume.

Divide the mixture between the 2 tins, smooth with a spatula – again, very gently – then bake for 7 minutes – no more than 8 – until the surface is very light gold in colour. Remove from the oven and flip each cake on to a cotton tea towel – you will find this sponge resilient. Peel off the parchment then take the shorter end and roll up immediately in the tea towel while hot. Allow to cool completely in the tea towel then wrap each whole roll in cling film.

Assemble the cake at least 1 hour before decorating. Line the square container or tin with cling film, making sure there is some overhang.

To make the buttercream filling, beat the butter until pale and creamy then gradually fold in the icing sugar. Continue to whip at high speed until airy and light, then beat in the vanilla and egg yolks.

Remove the cling film and cloth from each sponge, open out and spread with about 2mm of buttercream then a layer of jam – leave 3 tablespoons of jam to brush over the cake before icing. Roll the cakes up tight then pack into the lined tin, side by side.

To unmould, place a cake board on top and invert it. Lift off the tin then peel off the cling film.

To decorate, brush the top and sides of the cake with the reserved jam (you may need to liquidise it to make it smooth). Roll out the fondant icing to a 2mm thickness and drape it over the cake leaving the ends exposed. Trim 1cm/½ inch from the end to show off the layers inside, then decorate with crystallised flowers, sticking them to the surface using icing made from water and icing sugar.

Serves 10

Equipment

2 x 20x30cm/8x12-inch Swiss roll tins: butter the tins, line with baking parchment, then butter again and dust with flour

20cm/8-inch square container or cake tin at least 10cm/4 inches deep

Ingredients

For 2 Swiss rolls:

35g/1¼oz plain flour, sifted

23g/¾oz cornflour

4 eggs, plus 1 egg yolk

115g/4oz caster sugar

½ teaspoon vanilla extract

¼ teaspoon cream of tartar

For the filling:

250g/9oz softened butter

250g/9oz icing sugar

1 teaspoon vanilla extract

2 egg yolks

340g/12oz pot homemade or strawberry jam

To cover and decorate:

500g/1lb 2oz fondant icing, ready to roll

Crystallised rose petals or other edible flowers free from chemical sprays (see Suppliers, page 246)

Glacé icing, for sticking the flowers to cake: mix 50g/1¾oz icing sugar with 1–2 teaspoons water

Small

cakes

&

biscuits

Often it is the small things that look best on the counter. You can labour for hours on a layer cake or patiently make sourdough and brioche, but in the end eyes are always drawn to a stack of iced cakes or biscuits. The cupcake phenomenon says it all. Decoration draws the eye, initially, but what keeps us coming back for more is not what we see but the memory of the aroma and the flavour.

We have found that to make a great small cake you must begin with a search for a cake that pleases the palate and nose – and finally the eyes. A cupcake baker needs to keep changing the look of their cakes to attract customers, but the baker who can lodge a great memory of flavour will always have people coming back for more.

This devotion is linked to the origins of some famous biscuits, even those that are mass-manufactured. A chocolate digestive, for example, exemplifies the triumph of taste over looks. That is not to say we do not like to decorate and add colour to some cakes, and we make a cheerful, people-pleasing fairy cake, but the search for the winning biscuit or cakelet is unending.

Making small things has a demanding side. Small cakes are fiddly yet you need to work quickly or – from a baker's economical viewpoint – they represent labour for very little. They also, I have found too many times to my cost, cook so quickly they are vulnerable to mishaps.

Be more vigilant while baking small biscuits. A slight over-bake, biscuit edges that are a little too dark or cake middles too dry, are sadly a disaster. Where you can rescue a big cake by shaving off a singed edge and adding a bit of décor, biscuits and other small things promise a concentration of good taste and texture. If this is off-target, notice how they are abandoned by anyone who tries them.

You can avoid accidents by making a few rules for yourself: try to make your biscuits approximately the same size each time so that you instinctively get to know the period of cooking a certain favourite needs. Be consistent with the ingredients you use. Certain types or brands of butter or flour have particular characters. Fine-milled 'plain' flour varies from brand to brand in how it performs in baking; some flours are more finely milled, others absorb more liquid. These differences are small, and there is no need to recommend a particular brand, but you will have more success if you choose a type of flour or butter and use it consistently because the results will be more predictable.

MORE ABOUT BISCUITS

Timing. The speed at which many small things cook often means taking too many peeps at the activity in the oven. Each time the oven door is opened for checks, the heat drops and the cooking time must be extended, skewing future judgement on the right period needed to bake a tray of biscuits. Rely on a clockwork or electronic timer, set to ring an alarm about 3 minutes before the recommended cooking time.

Learn from first attempts. Because oven temperatures tend to vary, we have to get to know our ovens and how fast they bake. This is polarised when baking small things. If your oven bakes a biscuit in 10 minutes when the cooking time says 12, make a note. Keep a pencil close to your cookbook – the next time you make the biscuit in question might be weeks away and that little memo will be vital. Likewise if a biscuit is not cooked in the time given, note the number of minutes extra it actually did take.

Pale is good. Unlike pastry, where a 'high' bake brings out the flavour of the butter, for instance, aim for a paler tinge of gold with recipes in this chapter, unless specified. The important difference is to hold some of the moisture. We like our biscuits to be a little chewy or soft in the centre, and notice our customers prefer them that way, too. The ideal to aim for is a pale centre and a little colour around the edges.

Do not disturb the fresh-baked biscuit. Once out of the oven, allow to cool for a while without moving the biscuit. It will continue to cook for a bit on the tin (it is a good idea to use aluminium baking trays and bakeware, or simple tin, because the heat leaves the tin speedily) – then remove the baked items to a cooling rack.

Adding, taking away. We are aware that out there are millions of preferences and foibles. While the basics in recipes should stay unchanged: proportion of butter to flour/eggs/liquid, for example, feel free to play with other ingredients, alternating types of nuts, chocolate, fruit and other flavours. Make the biscuit or small cake you have always wanted; be creative and, if you make a mistake in this respect, clock it for the future – that is what makes a great confectioner.

Rare ingredients. The current great baking revival seems to be making great demands on our retailers. Supermarkets struggle to keep abreast of the latest craze in baking, but online suppliers seem ahead of the game. Sources of rare and unusual ingredients can be found in the back of this book (see Suppliers, page 246).

Brokens. The misshapen biscuit, the one that gets dropped, has its uses. Adopt a store of 'brokens' for adding to ice cream or Greek yoghurt. You put a lot of work into them – don't let them go to waste.

SCONES

The secret of a good scone is the flour. Plain white flour is often recommended in recipes but this produces a scone that has a cakey texture, when what we want is a bubbly, slightly tearable crumb. We prefer using strong white flour, which not only results in a high-rise scone but also provides the scones with a more lasting, lighter consistency. Going one step further and using a stone-milled strong white flour adds natural oils to the scone mixture, improving the quality further (see Suppliers, page 246).

One other very important tip for making great scones is to work quickly. As soon as the buttermilk or sour milk in the mixture comes into contact with the baking powder, it will react and create air bubbles. Therefore it is important to knead the dough only lightly and, when rolling before cutting, not to press down heavily. The faster you get from the mixing stage to the oven, the airier your scones will be. Leaving the dough hanging around will exhaust the activity in it.

Preheat the oven to 220°C/425°F/Gas mark 7. Put the flour in a bowl with the salt and whisk to distribute. Using your hands rub the butter into the flour until it resembles breadcrumbs. Add the baking powder and mix lightly but well with your hands. Add the buttermilk, mix with a spoon until it just about holds together and tip the mixture out on to a floured work surface. The dough will be wet and sticky.

Use floured hands or a dough scraper to lightly turn and knead the dough until you have a smooth ball. Do not worry if it is sticky. Keep the worktop well floured. Press the dough out with floured hands, or lightly roll to a thickness of 3cm/1¼ inches.

Dip the round cutter (or a knife if you have no cutters) in flour and then cut out the scones. Shake them out of the cutter and place on the lined baking sheet. Sprinkle over a little flour to keep the surface soft. Bake for about 15 minutes, or until pale golden and puffed to nearly double the size.

Variations

Ale and Cheddar cheese scones. Substitute 100ml/3½fl oz of the sour milk or buttermilk with ale, and add 150g/5½oz grated Cheddar or other cheese to the flour. Scatter grated cheese on the scones before baking. Eat with a ploughman's lunch of ham, pickle, salad and cheese.

Fresh goat's curd cheese and basil scones. Add 150g/5½oz of chèvre, cut into small pieces, and leaves from 4 sprigs of basil to the mixture with the flour.

Pancetta and sage scones. Chop 6 thin slices of pancetta into small strips and cook until crisp in a dry pan. Add the pancetta along with chopped leaves from 2 sprigs of sage, with the flour.

Raisin scones. Add 150g/5½oz raisins, previously soaked in a cup of black tea then drained, with the flour. This also works brilliantly with other dried fruit like figs, dates or apricots.

Raspberry and ricotta scones. Drain 250g/9oz pot of ricotta and leave on a plate in the fridge to dry for 2 hours. Cut into 1cm/½-inch lumps. Once the dough has come together, press it out into a rectangle, scatter over 150g/5½oz raspberries and the ricotta lumps. Fold the dough in 3, like a letter, then press with your hands to 4cm/1½ inches thickness and cut out the scones.

Makes 16–20

Equipment

8cm/3-inch round cutter

30cm/12-inch square baking sheet, preferably aluminium, lined with baking parchment, or a silicone baking mat

Ingredients

480g/1lb 1oz strong white stone-milled flour

1 teaspoon salt

90g/3¼oz cold butter, diced

15g/½oz baking powder

400ml/14fl oz buttermilk or milk soured with juice from half a lemon

OATCAKES

Why make oatcakes when almost every grocer, large or small, sells them? Well, it is time to meet the home-made oatcake, an altogether different character. Fragile, buttery and slightly puffed, this oatcake would never survive the rough and tumble of factory conveyor belts, transport, shelf-stacking and the long journey that takes an oatcake from oven to plate. For those times when the purchase of an especially beautiful piece of artisan cheese demands it, real oatcakes make the occasion splendid.

Use medium oatmeal to make oatcakes. You can also add a small quantity of pinhead oatmeal for a rough texture. Many oatcake recipes contain wheat flour because it makes the dough easy to handle. We like to keep ours pure, but include wholemeal spelt flour or a little rye for variation, if you want. To vary flavour, add dried herbs and spices like thyme, fennel seed or caraway seed.

Makes about 15–20

Equipment

2 x 30cm/12-inch square baking sheets, preferably aluminium, lined with baking parchment, or silicone baking mats (or bake in batches)

7cm/2½-inch round cutters (optional)

Ingredients

175g/6oz medium oatmeal

50g/1¾oz oat flour or rolled oats ground to a flour in food processor, plus extra for dusting

½ teaspoon baking powder

½ teaspoon salt

115g/4oz softened butter, diced

1 egg

1 egg yolk

1 tablespoon water

Preheat the oven to 180°C/350°F/Gas mark 4. Put the oatmeal, oat flour, baking powder and salt in a large bowl. Rub in the butter, stir in the egg, egg yolk and water and mix to a dough. Roll the dough into a cylinder 5cm/1¾-inch thick.

Cut 1cm/scant ½-inch discs from the dough, place them on an (oat) floured worktop and press them with your fingers to make a flatter biscuit about ½cm/¼ inch thick and 7cm/2½ inches across. If you want a perfect round make them a tiny bit larger than this and neaten them with a round cutter.

Use a palette knife to lift the oatcakes and place them 2cm/¾ inch apart on the baking sheets. Bake the oatcakes for about 8 minutes, until pale golden. Leave them to cool on the sheets. They will be fragile, so move them to the plate or tin carefully.

* If you buy jumbo oats, you must grind them to a medium-fine flour. Or use a combination of either fine and larger grains, or fine and medium oatmeal.

OATMEAL & FRUIT BISCUITS

A good mid-morning biscuit; you can omit the raisins and add nuts if you wish. Or combine both. You can also use muscovado instead of the soft brown sugar for a darker, less sweet biscuit, or substitute the raisins with sultanas, figs, chopped prunes or a combination of these.

Put the raisins and tea in a bowl for about 30 minutes to soften the dried fruit. Drain and set aside.

Combine the flour, cinnamon and salt in a bowl. Cream the butter in the stand mixer, beating it until fluffy and pale. Scrape down the sides from time to time. Add both sugars and continue to beat for about 4–5 minutes. Stir in the egg, then the vanilla, oats, raisins and flour by hand. Scoop the mixture out of the bowl and form into a long sausage, about 7cm/2½ inches across. Wrap in cling film and refrigerate for at least 30 minutes.

Preheat the oven to 170°C/325°F/Gas mark 3. Cut the dough sausage into 12 and place each disc on the baking sheet. Place them about 4cm/1½ inches apart on the baking sheet – they will expand during cooking. Bake for 15 minutes only. They should be pale brown and slightly darker at the edges and soft in the middle – the chewy softness in the centre is exactly the result you want.

Makes 12

Equipment

30cm/12-inch square baking sheet, preferably aluminium, lined with baking parchment, or a silicone baking mat

Ingredients

175g/6oz raisins

1 cup green tea, or Earl Grey

140g/5oz plain flour

2 teaspoons ground cinnamon

1 teaspoon salt

155g/5¾oz softened butter

140g/5oz soft brown sugar

65g/2½oz Demerara sugar

1 large egg, beaten

1 teaspoon vanilla extract

155g/5¾oz rolled oats

SPONGE FINGERS

Fresh from the oven, sponge fingers have lovely chewy centres and are nothing like those dry biscuits we buy in packets. You can also use them in trifles, tiramisu and charlottes, adding a more home-made character.

Equipment

2 x 30cm/12-inch square baking sheets, preferably aluminium, lined with baking parchment, or silicone baking mats (or bake in batches)

Piping bag with a 1cm plain round nozzle – or use a plastic bag with a hole snipped off the corner as a makeshift piping bag

Ingredients

35g/1¼oz plain flour

25g/1oz cornflour

4 eggs, separated

2 whole eggs

115g caster sugar, plus 2 teaspoons for the egg whites

5g/⅛oz vanilla extract

¼ teaspoon cream of tartar

To finish:

Extra caster sugar for dredging

Preheat the oven to 180°C/350°F/Gas mark 4. Sift the flour into a bowl, add the cornflour and whisk the two together. Use a stand mixer or hand whisk to whisk the egg yolks, whole eggs and sugar until pale cream-coloured and at least doubled in volume.

Add the vanilla, then sift half the flour mixture on to the surface and use a hand-held balloon whisk to gently, by dipping and lifting the mixture, fold it in. Sift in the remaining flour, and repeat the folding until all the flour is incorporated.

Whisk the egg whites for the cake – when they become foamy, add the cream of tartar. Once the eggs form soft white peaks of foam, add 2 teaspoons of sugar and continue to whisk until the peaks are very firm and glossy. Spoon the mixture into the piping bag and pipe 6 fingers on to each baking sheet, about 6cm apart. Dust with icing sugar, wait 5 minutes then dust with icing sugar again. This gives the fingers a pearly look.

Bake for 9–11 minutes until they are evenly pale brown. When the sponge fingers are done they will feel springy to the touch. Remove from the oven. Leave to cool on a wire rack, then store in an airtight container.

SHORTBREAD

The greatest buttery biscuit, when made as it should be. Do not, for that reason, skimp on the all-important butter. Buy one of those lovely yellow farmhouse-style butters; they make the shortbread more delicious.

Cream the butter in a stand mixer until pale and fluffy – you can also use a hand-held electric beater or do this in a bowl with a wooden spoon. Add the sugar and mix for a further 2 minutes. The mixture will still be gritty as granulated sugar does not dissolve in the butter when beaten. Add the vanilla and the flour, mixing slowly. Turn the mixture out on to the worktop and form into a ball, about 5cm/2 inches thick. Wrap in cling film and put in the fridge for 2 hours.

Preheat the oven to 170°C/325°F/Gas mark 3. To shape, tap the dough with a rolling pin on a lightly floured worktop, then roll to fit the tin. Use your hands to press the dough into the tin. Score in the places where you will cut or break it after cooking, making about 8 pieces of shortbread. Bake for about 20–30 minutes until pale brown. Cool in the tin for about 15 minutes then turn out carefully.

Makes 8 biscuits

. . . .

Equipment

A special 'petticoat tails' tin (see Suppliers, page 246) or a 23cm/9-inch round shallow baking tin. If using a tin with a detachable base, make sure you line it with baking parchment

. . . .

Ingredients

175g/6oz softened butter

90g/3¼oz granulated sugar

1 teaspoon vanilla extract

270g/9½oz plain flour

Extra caster sugar for sprinkling

FIG AND COBNUT 'NUDE' FLORENTINES

Nude means no chocolate – though you can immerse these lacy pleasures in a pool of melted chocolate once baked, if you wish. Without the chocolate, the caramelised nuts and fruit flavour are better appreciated. Traditionally Florentines are made with almonds and hazelnuts but with the revival of cobnuts (a relative of hazelnuts) in Kentish farms, adding them makes them a seasonal indulgence between August and October. Early in the season, cobnuts are 'wet' and have a milky, softer texture, making these a special variation on the traditional theme.

Makes about 12

....

Equipment

2 large baking sheets, lined with baking parchment (if you have one baking sheet, make these in 2 batches)

....

Ingredients

225g/8oz cobnuts or hazelnuts, shelled

105g/3¾oz butter

175g/6oz caster sugar

270ml/9½fl oz double cream

300g/10½oz flaked almonds

150g/5½oz dried Smyrna figs, cut into dice

100g/4oz sultanas

15g/¾oz plain flour, sifted

Preheat oven to 180°C/350°F/Gas mark 4.

Put the cobnuts or hazelnuts in a pan and dry-toast over a medium heat until fragrant. If the skins become loose, rub the nuts in a cloth to remove as much as you can. Roughly chop them and set aside.

Put the butter, sugar and cream in a pan and bring to the boil. Remove from the heat, add the flaked almonds, cobnuts or hazelnuts, figs, sultanas and sifted flour and mix very gently but thoroughly until well coated with the butter and sugar mixture.

Spoon a heaped tablespoon of the mixture on to the baking sheet, then spread it out to a circle about 8cm in diameter. There should be room for about 6 Florentines per baking sheet. Given that the mixture is lumpy, it is hard to say how thick the discs should be but approximately ½cm/¼ inch is ideal. If there are small gaps the size of your little fingernail, it does not matter – the sugar mixture will spread during cooking. Use a table knife to neaten the edges.

Bake for approximately 10–11 minutes until golden. You want them to be slightly darker gold around the edges. Allow to cool on the tray for several minutes before carefully transferring to a rack.

Giant Florentines

A nice way to finish a dinner party – make 2 large Florentines, measuring 21cm/8 inches – the size of a dessert plate. Bake as for the small Florentines; the centres will be paler than the edges. Cool on a rack and put on the table for guests to snap pieces from.

CARROT, OAT & ORANGE MUFFINS

A stand-in for breakfast with a wholesome, juicy crumb and the refreshing taste of orange. Use medium oatmeal, or rolled oats processed to a rough meal in a food processor.

Makes 12

Equipment

12-hole muffin tin lined with
12 paper cases

Ingredients

70g/2½oz medium oatmeal

225ml/8fl oz buttermilk

Zest of 1 orange

150g/5½oz grated carrot

125g/4½oz soft brown sugar

200g/7oz self-raising flour, sifted

1 teaspoon baking powder

2 tablespoons melted butter

2 eggs, beaten

For the icing:

100g golden icing sugar, sifted

4 teaspoons sieved orange juice

Preheat the oven to 220°C/425°F/Gas mark 7. Soak the oatmeal in the buttermilk for 30 minutes. Add the orange zest and carrot then mix well. Stir in the sugar, flour and baking powder and, when well incorporated, beat in the melted butter and eggs.

Spoon the mixture into the tin until it reaches ½cm/¼ inch from the top of the cases. Bake for 15–20 minutes, until the cakes are well risen and feel springy to the touch. Cool in the paper cases, placed on a rack.

Once the muffins are completely cool, make the icing. Add enough orange juice to the icing sugar to make a thick, pipe-able paste. Spoon the icing into a plastic food bag, forcing it into one of the corners at the base. Snip 1mm off the corner, and then pipe in a zigzag fashion across the surface of the cakes.

MASALA CHAI FRUIT CAKES

Dotted with raisins and sultanas that have been soaked in spiced Indian tea, these cakes have a nice sensibility and an old-fashioned tea time charm.

Preheat the oven to 180°C/350°F/Gas mark 4. Add the tea or teabags to 150ml boiling water. Put the dried fruit in a bowl and pour over the tea – through a strainer if necessary. Leave for 20 minutes, until the fruit is soft and plump, then strain, discarding the tea.

Put the syrup, sugar and butter in a small pan and heat slowly to boiling point. Allow to boil gently for 3 minutes until the mixture looks like soft and runny toffee. Remove from the heat and add the spices and tea-macerated fruit. Allow to cool for 5 minutes, then beat in the eggs. Sift in the flour, and mix well, then spoon the mixture into the tin, reaching about ½cm/¼ inch from the top of the paper cases.

Bake for 20 minutes, until the cakes look a little puffed and feel springy when pressed with a finger. Scatter over Demerara sugar while they are still hot, so it sticks to the surface of the cakes. Cool the cakes in their paper cases on a rack.

Makes 12

Equipment

12-hole muffin tin lined with 12 paper cases

Ingredients

2 teaspoons or 2 teabags masala chai (spiced Indian tea)

60g/2¼oz raisins

60g/2¼oz sultanas

115g/4oz golden syrup

115g/4oz Demerara sugar

115g/4oz butter

½ teaspoon ground cloves

½ teaspoon ground cinnamon

½ teaspoon ground ginger

2 eggs, beaten

250g/9oz self-raising flour

2–4 teaspoons Demerara sugar, to decorate

ROSEMARY & HONEY CAKES

A not-so-sweet but very delicious cake to bake in a square tray, then cut and paint each little cake with honey and lemon glaze. I use a strong-scented honey, like heather or lavender honey for flavour, which is even better accentuated with the aroma of rosemary.

Preheat the oven to 200°C/400°F/Gas mark 6. Put the butter and sugar together in a bowl and beat until pale and creamy. Gradually beat in the eggs then add the honey and rosemary leaves. Sift the flour, salt and spice together and fold into the mixture with the ground almonds until you have a smooth, golden batter.

Spoon the mixture into the cake tin and smooth the surface. Bake for 35–45 minutes, until the cake feels springy to the touch or a skewer inserted comes out clean. The cake will not rise very much; it has a lot of inner moisture and the ground almonds tend to weigh it down. Remove from the tin and leave to cool on a rack.

When cool, cut the cake into squares. To make the syrup, put the honey and the lemon juice in a pan and boil together for 1 minute to reduce. Paint the cakes all over with the syrup. Decorate with a little piece of honeycomb on each.

PISTACHIO AND LIME CAKES

The sweetness and amazing colour of unsalted pistachio with the exotic taste of lime in a soft cake that is pleasingly different to eat with a cup of coffee. You can either use unsalted pistachios, available from wholefood shops or Middle Eastern delis, or buy pistachio paste online (see Suppliers, page 246).

Preheat the oven to 220°C/425°F/Gas mark 7. Put the milk and lime juice in a jug and leave for a few minutes. The juice will sour and slightly thicken the milk. Set to one side.

Cream the butter and sugar until pale and light textured, then add the vanilla extract and lime zest. Beat in the eggs, then stir in the ground pistachios, almonds, flour and bicarbonate of soda, followed by the milk until you have a smooth batter.

Swiftly spoon the mixture into the muffin tin, filling the cases almost to the top (about ½cm/¼ inch below the top), then bake for 15–20 minutes until the cakes are well risen and feel springy to touch. Allow to cool in the paper cases, on a wire rack.

Mix together the icing sugar and caramel jam or dulce de leche until smooth. Spoon a little on to each cake and let it drip down the sides. Scatter over a few chopped pistachios on each cake to decorate.

Makes 12

Equipment

12-hole muffin tin lined with 12 paper cases

Ingredients

125ml/4fl oz milk

15ml/1 tablespoon fresh lime juice

60g/1¼oz softened butter

150g/5½oz soft light brown sugar

½ teaspoon vanilla extract

Zest of 2 limes

2 eggs, beaten

50g/1¾oz unsalted shelled pistachios, ground

50g/1¾oz ground almonds or pistachio paste

275g/9¾oz self-raising flour

½ teaspoon bicarbonate of soda

To decorate:

3 tablespoons sifted icing sugar

2 tablespoons caramel 'jam' or dulce de leche

2 tablespoons chopped unsalted shelled pistachios

CHOCOLATE BUTTERFLY CAKES

This style of cake takes me back to my childhood and making fairy cakes in our home kitchen, when we used to make butterfly cakes with vanilla sponge. Made with a lovely dark sponge, the tops of the cakes are levelled and the extra sponge divided and stuck, like wings, back on to the cake with a large dollop of chocolate buttercream. Roll over, cupcakes ...

Makes 20–24

....

Equipment

2 x 12-hole muffin tins (or bake in batches) and 24 paper cases

....

Ingredients

225g/8oz butter, diced

225g/8oz golden caster sugar

175g/6oz self-raising flour, sifted

50g/1¾oz cocoa powder, sifted

2 teaspoons baking powder, sifted

¼ teaspoon fine sea salt

1 teaspoon vanilla extract

4 eggs

100ml/3½fl oz milk

For the buttercream:

200g/7oz butter, softened

200g/7oz icing sugar, sifted

4 teaspoons cocoa, sifted

2 egg yolks

Little chocolate threads or hundreds and thousands, to decorate

Preheat the oven to 170°C/325°F/Gas mark 3. Place all the cake ingredients in a food processor and cream together – you will need to scrape the sides down from time to time. Spoon or pipe into the tin, filling the cases nearly to the top (½cm/¼ inch or so). Bake for 15 minutes or until well risen and springy when pressed. Remove from the oven and allow to cool. Make the second batch, if you are using one tin.

Meanwhile make the buttercream, beating all the ingredients together for about 5 minutes until the volume increases and the colour of the mixture lightens a little.

When the cakes are cool, cut the domed tops from them and pipe a generous blob of buttercream on top of the cake to completely cover the surface. Cut the tops of the cake in half to make two semicircles. Position them like a pair of wings and stick firmly into the buttercream.

GIANDUJA SANDWICHES

Two halves make an even better whole when filled with gianduja, the hazelnut-chocolate paste (pronounced gee-an-do-ya), invented in Turin, Northern Italy, two centuries ago. We love the versatility of these biscuits, which feel fresh after a generation of chocolate chip cookies. You can vary the filling by using white chocolate, almond and lemon; or a buttercream flavoured with caramel or mocha – or try mixing a couple of different fillings in one biscuit sandwich for added drama.

To make the biscuits, beat the butter and sugar together using a hand mixer until the mixture is light textured and pale in colour. Add the flour and condensed milk and mix until well combined. Remove the dough from the mixing bowl and form into a ball. Wrap in cling film and refrigerate for 30 minutes. (At this stage you can store the dough in the fridge for 2 days or in the freezer for 2 weeks.)

To prepare the gianduja filling, put the chocolate in a bowl set over a pan of gently simmering water making sure the base of the bowl does not touch the water. Stir as it melts, until you have a thin and smooth cream. Stir in the hazelnut paste or ground hazelnuts. Keep the mixture warm while the biscuits are baking.

Preheat the oven to 180°C/350°F/Gas mark 4.

Cut pieces from the dough, and roll into balls about the size of a walnut. Place on to the baking sheet, about 4cm apart (during cooking they will expand in size). Use your fingers or the back of a fork to flatten each ball slightly.

Bake for 10–12 minutes or until the edges of the biscuits are light brown in colour with centres that are pale and soft (the joy of these biscuits is their slightly chewy insides). Remove from the oven and leave to stand for about 3 minutes. Then gently transfer the biscuits using a palette knife to a rack to cool. When completely cool, spread a little of the warm gianduja on to the base of a biscuit round then gently sandwich together with another biscuit so that the filling does not escape. Allow the biscuits to set in a cool place. Dust with icing sugar for a little frosty beauty.

Makes 20 biscuits
to make 10 sandwiched biscuits

. . . .

Equipment

2 x 25cm x 30cm baking sheets, lined with baking parchment (or make these in 2–3 batches if you only have one baking sheet)

. . . .

Ingredients

225g/8oz unsalted butter

225g/8oz caster sugar

350g/12oz self-raising flour

100g/3½oz condensed milk

For the filling:

300g/10½oz milk chocolate, broken into pieces

100g/3½oz hazelnut paste or finely ground hazelnuts

Icing sugar for dusting

CHOCOLATE SQUARES

Very indulgent cakes made with melted chocolate, baked in a square then cut into pieces to have chocolate ganache spooned over them. I like to decorate these chocolate squares with the tiniest bit of gold.

Preheat the oven to 180°C/350°F/Gas mark 4. Put the chocolate in a bowl set over a pan of hot/simmering water and melt. Remove the bowl from the pan and allow to cool – don't wash this bowl up after use: you can use it again to melt the chocolate for the ganache glaze and the curls.

Put the butter and icing sugar in a stand mixer and beat well until pale and fluffy like buttercream. Beat in the egg yolks, one by one, then add the chocolate. Fold in the flour and salt until it is all incorporated. Set to one side.

Put the egg whites in a separate bowl with the salt, and whisk until foamy. Add the cream of tartar and then whisk until you have a white, soft foam or until you have reached soft peak stage. Add the caster sugar and whisk until the foam is stiff, glossy and white. Scoop this into the bowl with the chocolate mixture.

Using the large whisk attachment from the stand mixer, or a balloon whisk, fold the two mixtures together, slowly and gently dipping and lifting the whisk until it is all blended.

Pour the mixture into the tin, smooth the surface with a spatula then bake for 45–55 minutes until an inserted skewer comes out clean or the cake feels firm to the touch.

Leave to cool in the tin for a few minutes then turn out on to a board to cool completely. Meanwhile make the ganache. Chop the chocolate, and put it in a bowl. Heat the cream to boiling point then pour over the chocolate. After about 1 minute, stir until the chocolate melts and the mixture is smooth. Stop stirring as soon as you have the right consistency, and leave to cool for about 5–8 minutes.

Cut the cake into 5cm/2-inch squares (you should get 16 squares). Put them on a cooling rack and spoon some ganache over each one so the tops are well covered and the glaze drips down the sides. Add another spoonful if there is some left. Allow to set.

If making chocolate curls, melt the milk chocolate and allow it to cool to about 30–31°C. (If using dark chocolate, it should be 31–32°C; white chocolate 27–28°C.) Spread on a cool surface – a baking sheet or marble slab is ideal. Allow to set naturally, then use a palette knife to scrape the chocolate into curls. Place chocolate curls on each chocolate cake and add a little gold leaf, if you wish.

Makes 16

Equipment

20cm/8-inch square cake tin with loose base, buttered, the base lined with baking parchment then buttered and dusted with flour

Ingredients

240g/8½oz dark chocolate (minimum 70% cocoa solids), chopped

200g/7oz butter

165g/6oz sifted icing sugar

8 eggs, separated

185g/6¾oz plain flour, sifted

Pinch salt

¾ teaspoon cream of tartar

165g/6oz caster sugar

For the chocolate ganache:

200g/7oz dark chocolate, minimum 70% cocoa solids

200ml/7fl oz whipping cream

To decorate:

100g milk chocolate for the curls (optional)

Edible gold leaf (optional)

Waste

Not

It feels wrong to throw good bread away. When you know how much trouble goes into its making, disposing of it at the first sign of ageing feels wasteful. As it is, handmade bread and especially sourdoughs age in a different way to commercial bread. Enzyme softening agents, added to a typical 'sliced and wrapped' loaf, prolong the soft feeling of the bread for more than is natural. A preservative, such as citric acid, is also added, along with salt, but it is noticeable that mass-produced breads suddenly develop a rash of mould even when – weirdly – they still retain their soft and squidgy texture.

A bread made from all natural ingredients goes through a slower ageing process. It is true that the salt content will prevent moulds but the sourdough content also appears to combat decay. So the bread simply dries gradually over the days. When the texture is too dry to be fresh, it of course can be resurrected as toast, but this period of its life is the one I call 'twilight'– when the firm crumb and hard crust is better used as an ingredient in other dishes.

The economic argument for this, especially for those who buy rather than make artisan bread, is easily won. Why pay double or more for traditional handmade bread if half of it ends up in the bin? There's no doubt there is more pain in throwing away goods we spend more on. The beautifully made coat bought for a sizable amount of money will be worn and worn again, while that cheap and cheerful jacket from the high street chain, with which you were briefly smitten (and which probably frayed faster anyway), is dropped off at the charity shop without a backward glance.

It is a fact, anyway, that soft pappy bread does not lend itself well added to soups, pasta sauces or puddings in the same way that traditional bread will do. It turns to a spongy pulp when dipped in liquid, breaking apart. A sourdough, on the other hand, will hold its structure and even remain chewy. Dried to a crisp in the oven then mixed with tomatoes and olive oil, it becomes the meat of the dish. Soup made with stock from a leftover roast, ladled over slices of bread covered with grated cheese makes a nourishing meal, costing little.

Knowing how to use old bread is something of a lost convention, the paradox being that the easy availability of cheap factory-made bread taught cooks nothing about economy in the kitchen, while saving the money in our wallets. Getting to know how to use the remnants of a good loaf, storing fresh breadcrumbs in the freezer, keeping dry crumbs in a jar or enjoying the scent of an apple Charlotte toasting in the oven is as pleasurable as eating it freshly baked.

BREAD SALAD

Torn strips of flat bread or chunks taken from larger loaves can be dried in the oven and added to this olive oil-rich salad.

Serves 4

....

Ingredients

4 handfuls torn white bread

2 tablespoons black and green olives, pitted

1 tablespoon raisins

6 tablespoons olive oil

½ teaspoon salt

Juice of 1 lemon

1 teaspoon honey

2 tablespoons pine nuts, toasted in a dry pan until golden

300g small tomatoes, halved and deseeded

2 preserved artichoke hearts, quartered

2 roasted peppers, deseeded and cut into strips

2 courgettes, cut into sticks and briefly stir-fried to soften

2 large handfuls of parsley

4 anchovy fillets, cut into thin strips (optional)

4 eggs, boiled for 5 minutes then shelled and halved

Heat the oven to 180°C/350°F/Gas mark 4 and bake the bread pieces until pale gold – about 15–20 minutes.

Put the olives and raisins in a large bowl with the oil, salt, lemon and honey and leave to soak for 15 minutes. Add the pine nuts and all the remaining vegetables, with the bread. Drape over the anchovies and balance the egg halves over the top.

THE INSIDE–OUT SANDWICH

Layers of fresh summer vegetables and fresh goat's cheese, enclosing a single slice of sourdough bread, set into an elegant terrine. Whenever we have made this for bakery lunches, customers who prefer not to eat much bread have told us how much they love it.

Preheat the oven to 220°C/425°F/Gas mark 7. Place the red peppers, open side down on a baking tray lined with foil, and bake until the skin has blistered and blackened in places and the peppers are tender – about 30–40 minutes. Remove from the oven and put in a plastic bag, seal and leave to cool. Once cool, remove from the bags and peel off the skins.

Cut the courgettes into very thin slices, lengthways. The easiest way to do this is with a potato peeler, holding the courgette vertically so the slice falls on to the worktop. Heat the 2 tablespoons of oil for frying in a large frying pan and sauté the slices briefly on both sides so they soften but do not brown. Set to one side.

Using a knife, make a cross incision into the tomatoes and submerge in a bowl filled with boiling water. Leave for 2 minutes then drain. Peel the skins, cut the tomatoes in half and remove the seeds – do this in a sieve placed over a bowl so you catch the juice. Chop the tomato halves then put in the bowl with the juice. Add the 6 tablespoons of oil, basil and season with the salt and pepper. It is important to taste the tomato mixture to see if it needs more salt. Depending on the ripeness of the tomatoes, you may need more.

Now assemble the dish: line the loaf tin or mould with the courgette slices – laying them side by side, across the width of the dish. They should come up the sides, making a case for the other contents.

Spoon one quarter of the tomato mixture into the base of the dish; follow with two halves of roast pepper, laying them end to end to cover the tomato. Lay half of the cheese slices on top of the pepper, each piece touching the next one along the length of the mould. Spoon another quarter of the tomato on top of this, then place one layer of bread slices on top of the tomato, trimming them to fit the surface area of the mould.

To finish building the inside-out sandwich, add the remaining ingredients in reverse: first ¼ more of the tomato mixture, then the remaining cheese, then the other 2 roast pepper halves and finally the rest of the tomato mixture. Bring the cling film up to cover.

Cover the surface of the mould with aluminium foil, then place a weight on top – 2 cans of tomatoes are ideal. Refrigerate for several hours, or overnight. To unmould, carefully open up the cling film letting it fall down the sides of the mould. Place a plate or dish upside down on top and invert. Lift off the mould and carefully peel away the cling film. Cut slices 3cm/1¼-inch thick and lay them on their side so you can see the beautiful layers inside, including the tomato-soaked bread.

Serves 6

Equipment

20cm/8-inch loaf tin or terrine mould, lined with a large sheet of cling film

Ingredients

2 red sweet peppers, halved and deseeded

2 courgettes

2 tablespoons olive oil, for frying

8 plum tomatoes

6 tablespoons olive oil

12 basil leaves, shredded

1 teaspoon salt

½ teaspoon black pepper

250g fresh goat's cheese (a log or chèvre), sliced ½cm/¼-inch thick

2 large slices of sourdough bread, at least a day old

CRISPED BREAD, TO EAT WITH SOUP

There are a number of old and famed ways to eat ageing bread in soup: covered in toasted cheese with a dark onion broth spooned over then flashed under the grill, or – something the Italians are well known for – added to a broth with winter vegetables, beans, wholewheat spelt, black cabbage (cavolo nero), then boiled until you have a wonderfully thick comforting soup. I add bread in place of potato to smooth soups to thicken them, such as squash or tomato, but best of all, and beloved of children, are little torn-off chunks, fried first in oil with garlic and herbs. Croutons, to all that know them. We think they are a cut above the usual.

Serves 4

Ingredients

6 tablespoons olive oil

1 sprig sage

1 sprig rosemary

3 garlic cloves, crushed

6 handfuls of bread pieces, torn from the inside crumb of a loaf, at least 1 day old

Warm the oil with the herbs and garlic gently, leaving it to infuse for 15 minutes. Scoop out the garlic with a slotted spoon – it will burn, making the bread taste bitter, if left in. Raise the temperature to a medium heat and when the herbs begin to sizzle, add the bread. Fry until golden, turning regularly, then remove with a slotted spoon and drain on a kitchen cloth.

Add to soup straight away, or store these crisp breads in an airtight container until use – they will keep for a week. It is a nice idea to warm them a little in the oven before use.

GARLIC & PARSLEY BREADCRUMBS

To use instead of bread sauce, or sometimes in addition, when serving roast chicken, game birds, the Christmas turkey or roast pork.

Put all the ingredients except the parsley and 1 tablespoon of the melted butter into a pan and mix. Place over a low-medium heat. Gently fry, until the bread crisps up and the mixture becomes fragrant – add more butter if it looks too dry. Add the parsley and continue to stir-fry for a minute or two. Remove from the heat and transfer to a warm dish. Keep warm until the roast is served.

Toasted rye breadcrumbs
Rough, crumbled rye bread, toasted in a little oil until crisp, can be added to Nordic salads of smoked salmon and dill with a creamy honey mustard dressing.

Serves 4

Ingredients

12 tablespoons fresh sourdough breadcrumbs

Zest of 1 lemon

½ teaspoon ground allspice

¼ teaspoon grated nutmeg

60–75ml/4–5 tablespoons melted butter

4 heaped tablespoons chopped parsley

BREAD SAUCE

A bread sauce made with sourdough is like no other, because it adds an extra level of flavour. This is the one my mother taught me, and which I have taught my daughter Lara to make.

Put the milk in a pan. Stud the onion with cloves and add to the pan with the peppercorns and nutmeg. Bring the contents of the pan to boiling point and immediately remove from the heat. Leave to stand for at least an hour (when cooking ahead for big feasts, like Christmas, do this the day before and leave to infuse in the fridge). Strain the milk mixture and add almost all the breadcrumbs.

Stir, allowing the breadcrumbs to absorb the liquid. If the mixture seems too runny, add more breadcrumbs; too stodgy, add a little more fresh milk. Place over the heat and bring to simmering point. Cook for a minute – the bread will thicken the sauce. Add more or less at the last moment, should you need to, so you have a sloppy consistency. Add the cream and butter, then reheat. Season to taste and serve.

Serves 6

Ingredients

600ml/1 pint whole milk

1 onion, halved

10 whole cloves

6 peppercorns

A few gratings of nutmeg

6 handfuls fresh breadcrumbs, plus more in reserve

4 tablespoons double cream

2 nuts of butter

Salt

APPLE CHARLOTTE

Of all the puddings made with bread, this – along with summer pudding – is my favourite. You rarely see an old-fashioned Charlotte, made in a pretty, shallow ovenproof dish, the surface of the pudding golden toasted and inviting. Use day-old white bread slices, cut nice and thin, for this pudding.

Serves 6–8

Equipment

Ovenproof dish,
about 1 litre/1¾-pint capacity

Ingredients

6 cooking apples, peeled,
cored and sliced

30g/1oz butter

½ teaspoon ground cinnamon

Zest and juice of half a lemon

2–4 dessertspoons light brown
sugar, or to taste

8 thin slices bread, at least a
day old but not too dry, cut into
5cm/2-inch triangles

200ml/7fl oz melted butter

Demerara sugar for dusting

Double cream for serving

Preheat the oven to 200°C/400°F/Gas mark 6. Put the apples in a pan with the butter, cinnamon, lemon zest and juice. Cook until the apples are tender but not mushy then add enough sugar to sweeten. Transfer the apple mixture to the ovenproof dish. Dip the bread triangles in the melted butter then arrange them on the surface of the pudding, side by side and overlapping. Bake until the surface of the Charlotte is golden and crisp. Remove from the oven and dust with Demerara sugar. Serve with thick, yellow double cream.

USEFUL SUPPLIERS & RESOURCES

Sourdough baking equipment

Bakery Bits

www.bakerybits.co.uk

1 Orchard Units,
Duchy Road,
Honiton,
Devon, EX14 1YD, UK
Tel: 0044 (0) 1404 565656

Bertinet Kitchen

www.thebertinetkitchen.com

12 St Andrew's Terrace,
Bath, BA1 2QR, UK
Tel: 0044 (0) 1225 445531

AJ Stuart

(dough trays)

www.ajstuart.co.uk

161 Dargan Crescent,
Belfast, County Antrim
BT3 9JP, Northern Ireland
Tel: 0044 (0) 28 9077 6808

USA

San Francisco Baking Institute

www.sfbi.com

480 Grandview Drive,
South San Francisco,
CA 94080, USA
Tel: 001 650 589 5784

Bakeware

Lakeland

www.lakeland.co.uk
Tel: 0044 (0)1539 488 100

John Lewis

www.johnlewis.com

Tel: (from the UK) 08456 049
049; (from overseas) 0044
(0) 1698 545454

Flour

Stoate & Son

*(supplier of organic strong white
and rye flour to Pocket Bakery)*

www.stoatesflour.co.uk

Cann Mills

Shaftesbury,
Dorset, SP7 0BL, UK
Tel: 0044 (0) 1747 852475

Shipton Mill

www.shipton-mill.com

Long Newnton,
Tetbury,
Gloucestershire, GL8 8RP, UK
Tel: 0044 (0) 1666 505050

Doves Farm

www.dovesfarm.co.uk

Doves Farm Foods Ltd,
Salisbury Road,
Hungerford,
Berkshire, RG17 0RF, UK
Tel: 0044 (0) 1488 684880

Leckford Estate Flour

Available in-store from
Waitrose branches

Bacheldre Watermill

www.bacheldremill.co.uk

Bacheldre Watermill,
Churchstoke,
Montgomery,
Powys, SY15 6TE, UK
Tel: 0044 (0) 1588 620489

Gilchesters Organics

(rare breed wheat flour/spelt)

www.gilchesters.com

Gilchesters Organic Farm,
Hawkwell,
Northumberland NE18 0QL, UK
Tel: 0044 (0)1661 886 119

Sharpham Park

(spelt flour)

www.sharphampark.com

Street,
Somerset, BA16 9SA, UK
Tel: 0044 (0)1458 844080

Forno Bravo

(Italian Caputo '00' flour)

www.fornobravoukshop.co.uk

Tel: 0044 (0)1206 831 985

Casa Julia

*(Italian Caputo '00' flour, fine
sea salt)*

www.casajulia.co.uk

11 Springwood Drive,
Braintree, Essex, CM7 2YN, UK

Tel: 0044 (0) 1376 320269

USA

L'Epicerie

www.lepicerie.com

106 Ferris Street,
Brooklyn,
New York, NY 11231-1094, USA
Tel: 001 718 596 7575

Miscellaneous ingredients

Bakery Bits

(sourdough starter and yeast, essences, nibbed sugar and candied fruit)

www.bakerybits.co.uk

1 Orchard Units,
Duchy Road,
Honiton,
Devon, EX14 1YD, UK
Tel: 0044 (0) 1404 565656

Fortnum & Mason

(fresh grocery/storecupboard ingredients)

www.fortnumandmason.com

181 Piccadilly,
London, W1A 1ER, UK
Tel: (from the UK) 0845 300
1707; (from overseas) 0044 (0)
207734 8040

Low Sodium Sea Salt Company

www.soloseasalt.com

103 Palace Road,
Bromley,
Kent, BR1 3JZ, UK
Tel: 0044 (0) 20 8464 1665

Why Nut

(pistachio and other nut pastes)

www.whynut.co.uk

48 Deardon Way,
Shinfield,
Reading, RG2 9HF, UK
Tel: 0044 (0) 7879 658041

Netherend Farm

(butter)

www.netherendfarmbutter.co.uk

Woodside, Woolaston,
Lydney,
Gloucestershire GL15 6PB, UK
Tel: 0044 (0) 1594 529484

Clarence Court Farm

(eggs with bright yellow yolks from traditional breeds)

www.clarencecourt.co.uk

Tel: 0044 (0) 1579 345718

Contact for stockists/
Waitrose branches

Natoora

(fresh grocery; rare citrus including bergamot, cedro, Amalfi lemons)

www.natoora.com

Unit 8 Discovery Business Park
St James's Road,
London, SE16 4RA, UK
Tel: 0044 (0) 20 7627 1600

Daylesford Organic

(organic farmhouse cheeses, eggs, milk, meat)

www.daylesfordorganic.com

Tel: 0044 (0) 1608 731700

Farm shop,
Daylesford, near Kingham,
Gloucestershire, GL56 0YG, UK

Plus London branches

Decorations

Fortnum & Mason

(edible flower petals, coloured and flavoured sugar)

www.fortnumandmason.com

181 Piccadilly,
London, W1A 1ER, UK
Tel: (from the UK) 0845 300
1707; (from overseas) 0044
(0)20 7734 8040

Jane Asher Sugarcraft

www.janeasher.com

22–24 Cale Street,
London SW3 3QU, UK
Tel: 0044 (0) 20 7584 6177

Squires Kitchen

(couverture chocolate, quality cocoa, colouring pastes, marzipan and decorations)

www.squires-shop.com
Tel: 0044 (0) 1252 260260

Meadowsweet Flowers

(crystallised flowers)

www.meadowsweetflowers.co.uk
Tel: 0044 (0) 1598 740494

Limeslake Farm

South Molton,
Devon, EX36 3LY, UK

Hope & Greenwood

(traditional confectionery)

www.hopeandgreenwood.co.uk

Various London locations:

20 North Cross Road,
London, SE22 9EU, UK;

1 Russell Street,
Covent Garden,
London, WC2B 5JD, UK

Tel: 0044 (0) 20 8613 1777

Marchesi di San Giuliano

www.marchesidisangiuliano.it

Tel: 0039 0931 959022

Ortigia

(Sicilian organic citrus fruits in syrup)

55 Sloane Square,
London, SW1, UK

Tel: 0044 (0)20 7730 2826

Bread-making &
baking courses

School of Artisan Food

(diploma and short courses)

www.schoolofartisanfood.org

Lower Motor Yard,
Welbeck,
Nottinghamshire, S80 3LR, UK

Tel: 0044 (0) 1909 532171

Daylesford Cookery School

www.daylesfordorganic.com

Daylesford, near Kingham,
Gloucestershire, GL56 0YG, UK

Tel: 0044 (0) 1608 731620

Bertinet Kitchen Cookery School

www.thebertinetkitchen.com

12 St Andrew's Terrace,
Bath, BA1 2QR, UK

Tel: 0044 (0) 1225 445531

Lighthouse Bakery School

www.lighthousebakery.co.uk

Ockham, Dagg Lane,
Ewhurst Green,
Robertsbridge,
East Sussex TN32 5RD, UK

Tel: 0044 (0) 1580 831271

Organisations

The Real Bread Campaign

www.realbreadcampaign.org

Flavour First

www.flavourfirst.org

Pocket Bakery Bread

Wholesale/retail

www.pocketbakery.org

Pocket Bakery bread wholesale

Bread Bread, Unit 37, Mahatma
Ghandi Estate, Milkwood Road,
London, SE24 0JF, UK

Tel: 0044 (0) 20 7733 7675

**Our bread is also available from
Fortnum & Mason**

www.fortnumandmason.com

181 Piccadilly,
London, W1A 1ER, UK

Tel: (from the UK) 0845 300
1707; (from overseas) 0044 (0)
20 7734 8040

INDEX

ACKNOWLEDGEMENTS

My thanks to all at Orion Publishing who have worked so hard and patiently on this book, especially Amanda Harris and Kate Wanwimolruk, and also to my friend Jacks Thomas for all her encouragement. I am very grateful to have worked with Laura Hynd again, whose photography is as beautiful as ever.

It is right to say, though, that this book is not just mine but also belongs to my children and my husband Dominic. Their perseverance with the bakery has been amazing. Finally I would like to dedicate the book to our customers who have been with us from the start, and without which the Pocket Bakery would never have thrived.

– Rose Prince, 2013

First published in Great Britain in 2013
by Weidenfeld & Nicolson, an imprint
of Orion Publishing Group Ltd

Orion House, 5 Upper St Martin's Lane,
London WC2H 9EA
An Hachette UK company

10 9 8 7 6 5 4 3 2 1

Text copyright © Rose Prince 2013

Design and layout © Weidenfeld & Nicolson 2013

A CIP catalogue record for this book is available
from the British Library.

ISBN: 978-0-297-86938-2

Design and lettering by Sinem Erkas

Photography by Laura Hynd

Props styling by Polly Webb-Wilson

Home economist assistant: Katy Ross

Copy-edited by Mari Roberts

Printed and bound in China

The Orion Publishing Group's policy is to use papers that
are natural, renewable and recyclable products and made
from wood grown in sustainable forests. The logging and
manufacturing processes are expected to conform to the
environmental regulations of the country of origin.

www.orionbooks.co.uk